The
Wildest Colts
make the
Best Horses

By John Breeding, Ph.D.

Published By:
BRIGHT BOOKS, INC.
2313 Lake Austin Boulevard, Austin TX 78703
(512) 499-4164

Printed in the U.S.A.

Library of Congress Catalog Card Number: 96-85810

ISBN 1-880092-39-5

ACKNOWLEDGMENTS

Polly Nance, without whose hard work and joyful devotion to producing this manuscript, this book could never have happened at this time in my life.

Marilyn Waitt, whose excellent editing greatly improved the quality of this book.

Jerry Boswell, for the inspiration of his fighting spirit.

Ginger Ross and Peter Breggin, for their passionate, eloquent and painstakingly researched defense of children's souls against the relentless, dangerous onslaught of BioPsychiatry. Their work guides much of my thinking on the subject matter of this book.

Kelly Jackson, John Jarrett, and Andrew Prough for all their help in publishing the booklet which is the father of the book.

Themistocles Z(524?-460? BC), for the title of this book, quoted in Peter Breggin's *Toxic Psychiatry*, p. 269. The original citation, given to me by Leonard Frank, is *Plutarch's Lives*, Dryden Edition, 1673.

Dan Jones, for his wonderful song to himself, *Shameless*.

Bill Jeffers, for his poem *Don't Be Nice* which so captures the spirit of this book, and for his design and layout of this book and its cover.

Patty Wipfler, for her magnificent parenting work which I share in Appendix A.

Diane Shisk, for *Beloved Child, You Are Wanted,* a beautiful reminder of what children need to hear from us.

Leonard Roy Frank, for his encouragement and inspiration. I am especially grateful for his appendix of quotations on children, a dessert that I know you will enjoy.

My heartfelt thanks also go out to the following family and friends who have contributed financially to help make this "Wildest Colts" work possible: Ed and Ruth Anne Breeding, Anne Smith and Vickery Wholesale Nursery, Moira Dolan, M.D., Don and Grace Ertel, Betty Anderson, Jim Frederick, Susan Breeding, Tom Breeding, Raquel Fuentes, Bob and Beth Green, Larry and Gloria Green.

DEDICATION

To my children, Eric and Vanessa, for the intense demand of their spirited natures which has forced me, kicking and screaming to transform myself and my life in ways I could never have imagined, again and again and again. . .

Old Camelback was a highly successful gardener. People wanted to know the secret of his success, but he denied having any particular method other than fostering natural tendencies, that is, forwarding life. He said, "In planting trees, be careful to set the roots straight, to smooth the earth around, to use good mould and to ram it down well. Then, don't touch the trees, don't think about them, don't go and look at them, but leave them alone to take care of themselves and nature will do the rest. I only avoid trying to make trees grow—others are forever running backwards and forwards to see how they are growing, sometimes scratching them to make sure they are still alive, or shaking them to see if they are sufficiently firm in the ground, thus constantly interfering with the natural bias of the tree and turning their affection and care into an absolute bane and curse. I only don't do these things. That's all."

Chuang Tze

Table Of Contents

INTRODUCTION

IN the spring of 1994, a female client came to my office for a counseling session; she had just left her son's school. The boy's teacher told this young mother that her boy was having some problems in the classroom and expressed her concern that he was showing symptoms of "Attention-Deficit Hyperactivity Disorder" (ADHD). The teacher informed this mother that her son was somewhat disruptive and recommended that she seek a medical consultation for the boy. The teacher gave my client some literature on "attention-deficit hyperactivity disorder" and a list of referral names. She assured this young mother, who has little money, that the state (Medicaid) would pay for this important medical help.

When my client began to ask questions, the teacher pointed out the boy's cluttered desk—a "symptom" of this "disease." She asked if it was hard to get the boy's attention when he watched television. The mother's yes answer revealed this as another "symptom" of the "disease." The teacher gave her a checklist of "symptoms" including "frequency of climbing behavior" (too much climbing was another symptom).

The National Institute of Mental Health informs us that one out of 10 young boys "suffers from" this dreaded disease. An estimated two million take Ritalin, which our Drug Enforcement Administration classifies as Class II along with morphine, barbiturates and other prescription drugs that have a high potential for addiction or abuse. The so-called "side effects" of Ritalin include sadness, depression, social withdrawal, flattened emotions and loss of energy. Long-term use tends to create the very same problems that Ritalin is supposed to combat—attentional disturbances, memory problems, irritability and hyperactivity.

So, according to current psychiatric thought, a high activity level, playful interaction with peers in the classroom, a cluttered desk, difficulty getting a boy's attention while he is watching television (I have never met anyone for whom this is not true) and too much climbing are all indications of a psychiatric disorder.

Something is seriously wrong here! Hundreds of thousands of children, mostly boys, are being forced to take dangerous drugs—not because they have suffered or are suffering from a dreaded medical disease, but because we, as a society, have chosen to turn normal behavior (activity, energy, zest, spirit, absorption in television, climbing, challenging authority—which is demanding you do something you are not interested in or ready for) into "symptoms" of a "disease."

It used to be these boys were considered incorrigible or bad (sinful); theology was used to coerce, punish, control, and demand conformity. Now it is done in the name of medical science; institutional psychiatry is used to control and coerce. These boys are no longer bad; now they are sick, suffering from a "disease."

The view of those people who promote these ideas is that we can help them with drugs. It just so happens that those same people can make an enormous profit while doing so much good.

I felt that my session with this young woman saved a child from the "psychiatric police." I wrote a letter to the editor of the local newspaper describing the above experience. This letter initiated an unexpected chain of events that has resulted in the book you are now reading. My letter evoked many calls and a controversial series of letters on both sides of this ADHD issue. On January 13, 1995, the *Austin American-Statesman* published an editorial by me entitled "Widespread Misuse of Ritalin Is a National Disgrace." The controversy became even more heated. One frequent response I got, sometimes in a friendly tone and sometimes in an accusatory one, was, "Well, what are your solutions then?" In response to this I wrote a booklet called *The Wildest Colts Make The Best Horses.* The little colt of a booklet, born out of my struggle to respond to what I see as a tragic and unfortunate situation, has grown into this book.

Contrary to the popular homily, this is one book you can tell by its cover. The title, *The Wildest Colts Make The Best Horses,* conveys an attitude that ennobles and supports an effort to defend and enhance the spirits of our young people. The subtitles also communicate a great deal of information.

The first subtitle, *The truth about Ritalin, "ADHD" and other "disruptive behavior disorders"* reveals that the book addresses at length the specific phenomenon of labeling huge numbers of our children with these diagnoses and giving these children drugs. As suggested by the second subtitle, *"What to do when your child is labeled a problem by the schools,"* this book is very much oriented toward parents[1] or other adults who need support with this issue. The book holds a great deal of information that is generally useful to adult allies of young people in any situation.

---

[1] For practical reasons I orient this book toward parents. If you are a teacher or other adult ally of young people, please include yourself, as I include you in my thinking. The principles are the same.

I have divided the book into three major sections.

Part I: RECOGNITION AND REMEMBRANCE. To respond effectively to a situation, we need a realistic picture of that situation. In my view, our society greatly distorts reality in regard to the experience of young people and schools. Specifically, I address the practice of what I call BioPsychiatry (i.e., the reduction in our thinking about human beings to biological and genetic function and the subsequent use of drugs and/or electric shock to "treat" that function). Recognizing and understanding BioPsychiatry is crucial to effectively respond to the fact that we have about two million children on Ritalin today in the United States and to deal with the pressures we receive to drug our own children. The section on RECOGNITION also presents ideas that I think are important to realize about schools and a few key beliefs that influence the way we relate to our children.

This part of the book is also about REMEMBRANCE. It is extremely challenging to be a parent under any circumstance (or to be a parent surrogate such as a teacher or other adult caregiver). Our society is not set up to effectively support those who care for our young. It is even more challenging, and often overwhelming, to be a parent when your child is having a hard time or not "acting right." When others, such as school and mental health authorities, are pressuring you to do something about your child's problems, the stress becomes even more intense. I think that at these times we are most likely to forget who we *really* are, who our child *really* is, and what is *really* important. My goal in this section is to provide a few reminders toward re-remembering the true nature of your child and of yourself as a parent. I also provide a few pointers to hold onto during this stressful time.

Part II: INFORMATION AND ACTION. This section covers several areas that respond to that original question of "What are your solutions then?" The emphasis of this section is on Action — what else you can do as a parent to help your child. My experience was that I got precious little good information to prepare me for my role as a parent. I am very aware of how extremely difficult it is to implement the ideas I present in the face of our distressed society. I hope that what I offer here will help you respond to the challenge of parenting and being good allies to our young people.

I have chosen to alternate gender pronouns at will, especially in describing children, rather than attempt to neuter, pluralize or simply use the masculine for convenience sake. It is my view that sex differences need not affect parenting decisions except when determining how best to counter the heavy gender conditioning that comes down on boys and girls in their respective cultures.

Part III: ON COUNSELING CHILDREN. This section contains the heart of what I offer in this book. I know that the theory I present here is a tremendous affront to much of the conventional wisdom and conditioned thinking with which we are all thoroughly saturated. I also know it is a tremendous challenge to implement this approach in the face of what I call parental oppression and lack of support for children, parents and families in our society. Therefore I go into some depth on key areas including shame, crying, fear and anger. In addition, I share my own experience as a parent, particularly some of the trials, tribulations and successes I've had with my son, Eric. I humbly offer the teachings that have been helpful to me with the caveat that this is one *father who does not know best.*

PART I

Recognition and Remembrance

CHAPTER 1
About BioPsychiatry

The Illusionary Veil

About two million school-age children are on Ritalin in the United States today. We can only guess at how many more children manage to avert drug use like my client's son I told you about in the Introduction. I do know from my own parenting workshops and consulting work that parents receive immense pressure to put their children on psychoactive drugs. I also know from this work that *many* parents do a tremendous job of courageously resisting this pressure. It is safe to say that, for every child put on drugs, there are many more who would be if not for valiant parent resistance.

In order to see something clearly, it is necessary to remove any veil that covers or obscures it. BioPsychiatry is such a veil and merits our critical examination.

Young people today are brought into our mental health system literally by the millions. Significant entry points into this system appear to be around key transitions or passages into new levels of societal demand. It is becoming a well-known observation that as a society we fail to help our young people make a successful passage into adulthood. Youth despair is massive. Suicide rates for adolescents have nearly tripled since 1950, a clear indicator of our failure. Colt (1991) points out that "advances in medicine have lowered the mortality rate for every age group in America, except fifteen to twenty-four-year olds, whose rate has risen, largely because of the increase in suicides. (300% increase in suicide rate for ten to fourteen year olds.)" Major breakdowns, or simply the failure to become *productive* members of society during this challenging passage from adolescence into young adulthood, are considered signs or symptoms of mental illness. Treatment begins.

My observation is that, in the case of Ritalin and ADHD, there are two major portals into the mental health system. The first is entry into elementary school. Hundreds of thousands of five, six and seven-year-old children are diagnosed, labeled and "treated" with drugs. Entry into middle school and/or junior high is the second major portal. Extremely large numbers of young people flounder during this transition. Very many are then introduced to the mental health system. Many more, already initiated, go deeper into the system.

These are facts about a large-scale, societal phenomenon. Millions of children and parents go through a specific, singular experience. Johnny enters school and somehow it does not go well. Although his learning and even his grades may be fine, somehow he doesn't act right. He is seen as restless and distractible, or vague and spacey. Sometimes it's the other way around. He is polite and cooperative, but he doesn't learn. More often he learns, but is unorganized or doesn't seem to care about turning in his work, so he gets bad grades.

Johnny's teacher, Ms. Jones, is concerned. She may or may not be frustrated or irritated; she is definitely concerned. Like virtually all teachers today, she has been introduced through a class or workshop to mental health system information about the identification and treatment of ADHD. Most likely, the information she received included dramatic case illustrations presented as modern, up-to-date, clinical scientific research emphasizing diagnostic criteria and symptomatology. With easy-to-use behavioral checklists provided as screening devices, the importance of referral and evaluation by a trained mental health professional was stressed. She was no doubt told that Ritalin has been shown to be safe and effective in treating many children with this disease.

In her workshop, Ms. Jones learned that the official standard for ADHD as defined by the Diagnostic and Statistical Manual (DSM) of the American Psychiatric Association requires any eight of 14 items. The first five items are described as most useful:

1. Often fidgets with hands or feet or squirms in seat (in adolescence, may be limited to subjective feelings of restlessness).
2. Has difficulty remaining seated when required to do so.
3. Is easily distracted by extraneous stimuli.
4. Has difficulty awaiting turn in games or group situations.
5. Often blurts out answers to questions before they have been completed.
6. Has difficulty following instructions.
7. Has difficulty sustaining attention to tasks.
8. Often shifts from one uncompleted activity to another.
9. Has difficulty playing quietly.
10. Often talks excessively.
11. Often interrupts or intrudes on others.
12. Often does not seem to listen.
13. Often loses things necessary for tasks.
14. Often engages in physically dangerous activities without considering consequences.

This teacher was also taught that ADHD is a specific "mental illness" with a genetic and biochemical cause. As a member of the public, she has been exposed repeatedly to media information such as a recent Associated Press wire article with a headline stating that "Attention deficit disorder plagues two million kids." The article poses the question: "What is attention deficit disorder?" The answer: "It is a biochemical condition that affects school-age children and is characterized by a short attention span."

Ms. Jones was also shown how to use behavioral checklists. The resident Austin authority on ADHD recommends two checklists in her workshops. The first involves ratings of severity on problems with attending and concentrating in various situations such as individual work, group activities, free time and field trips. The second, called ADHD Rating Scale, is a four point ("Not at all" to "Very much") rating of the exact fourteen behaviors listed above from the *Diagnostic Manual of the American Psychiatric Association.*

Ms. Jones is concerned about Johnny. She has evaluated him according to the criteria on her behavioral checklists. She calls his parents in for a conference, expresses her concerns and offers her opinion that he may have ADHD. She emphasizes that she is not a mental health professional and recommends that they take Johnny in for an evaluation by a psychiatrist to make an official diagnosis. There may be an intermediary referral to a non-medical professional lower in the mental health hierarchy, perhaps even working within the school. This professional will then evaluate Johnny and subsequently refer him to a psychiatrist for medical considerations. Many parents understandably trust and immediately defer to the opinions and advice of these trained professionals.

Those who resist often experience tremendous pressure to "do what's best for your child" and give him the medication he needs for his disease.

BioPsychiatry is the institutionalized practice of selecting individuals on the basis of appearance and behavior, identifying them as mentally ill, and treating them with drugs and/or electroshock. BioPsychiatry is based on a very specific set of guiding principles that are as follows:

(1) Adjustment to society (school) is good.

(2) Failure to adjust is the result of mental illness (ADHD).

(3) Mental Illness (ADHD) is a medical disease.

(4) Mental Illness (ADHD) is the result of biological and/or genetic defects.

(5) Mental Illness (ADHD) is incurable.

(6) Mental Illness (ADHD) can be controlled primarily by drugs, secondarily, for really serious mental illness, by electroshock.

With these assumptions in mind, I will now examine the mechanisms by which BioPsychiatry enforces its position and interferes with (cloaks) our ability to see the truth of what is going on. The first mechanism is most profound. It suppresses the natural process, addressed in detail later in this book, by which people resolve emotionally charged experiences. The core of institutional psychiatry is the suppression of emotional expression. Mainstream (meaning the agencies of the economically, politically and socially powerful in society) mental health practices center around systematic inhibition of emotional expression.

The heart of current BioPsychiatry practice is psychopharmacology. Other control patterns range from seemingly benevolent (psychotherapy attempts to soothe away "too much crying") to cruel and severely damaging practices such as electroshock and psychosurgery. Psychiatry's physical treatments (drugs, shock and psychosurgery) are often used coercively and almost always without genuine informed consent. Much of children's problematic (disrupting or otherwise not adjusting to classroom expectations) behavior may be seen as an attempt on the part of these children to show where they have been hurt and to express emotions associated with having been hurt. Drugging children sends a very clear message and acts as a powerful suppressant of emotional expression.

The second mechanism by which BioPsychiatry obscures reality involves a trick of magic or sleight of hand. The mechanism is indirection and illusion. "Now you see it, now you don't." "Before you get a glimpse of social injustice, let me show you mental illness." "Before you think about racism and economic injustice, let me show you genetic predisposition to violence in young black males." Institutional psychiatry has been so successful in their magic show that few people realize that "mental illness" is, at best, merely a metaphor. To quote Peter Breggin (1994), foremost writer and outspoken challenger of the tenets of BioPsychiatry: "It is scientifically incontrovertible that there is no convincing evidence that any condition routinely seen by psychiatrists has a genetic or biological origin." (p. 188) The concept of mental illness was originally created as a metaphor in order to establish medical/scientific credibility for the accepted practices of responding to people in distress or in deviance from social norms.

I presented the ADHD checklists in some detail to clearly show that the criteria for this alleged disease are strictly social and behavioral—no blood tests, urine tests, tissue samples, x-rays, etc. ADHD is not diagnosed by medical tests. Mental illness is a metaphor; ADHD is a metaphor saying that this behavioral phenomenon is a medical disease. Let me illustrate with two metaphors.

- Johnny runs fast and swift, a deer runs fast and swift; Johnny is a deer.
- Johnny is restless and inattentive to school tasks, a person with organic brain syndrome is restless and inattentive; Johnny is a medical disease (ADHD).

As Diane McGuinness (1989) reports in her thoroughly researched chapter on Attention Deficit Disorder, "the emperor has no clothes." She convincingly demonstrates the absence of any valid diagnostic procedure, as well as the failure of drug therapy to facilitate any academic, social or emotional well-being for the child. She thoroughly debunks the notion that research on ADHD bears any approximation to neutral, "pure" scientific research. The initial impact of stimulant drugs on behavior makes it very difficult to dislodge medical practitioners and other believers from their point of view. The truth is, however, as McGuinness concludes, that "the data consistently fail to support any benefits from stimulant medication." Harmful effects continue to be minimized.

The agency of BioPsychiatry is performing the greatest magic show on earth. The incredible illusion of biologically caused mental illness serves as a powerful enforcer of oppression, consistently distracting our attention from the reality of social injustice and the devastating results on individuals and society. BioPsychiatry says that two million children have a medical disease called ADHD. I say there is a need to look at the schools, at families, at community, at all the social justice issues involved in how we care for young people in our society. I'll give you a hint now on one key to see through this illusion. ADHD is "big business." Keep your eye on where the money goes. Or as investigative journalists are advised, "Follow the money."

The third way that BioPsychiatry acts to prevent close examination of our situation with the care of our young has a much more elastic quality, adapting to specific groups and individuals. It really doesn't function as a clear universal symbol; I think it's more like law enforcement. It is hard to get hold of because the laws, though well-known, are unwritten. They are the laws of oppression, the laws of adultism, racism, sexism, heterosexism, anti-Semitism, etc. The mechanism is simple. If a person steps outside the bounds of the oppressive conditioning (i.e., fails to act in the way that a child, woman, man, person of color, etc., is supposed to act), then the agents of institutional psychiatry are available to punish her for her transgression, enforcing her prescribed role. If a child doesn't act right and produce in school, label her mentally ill and give her drugs.

Piercing the Veil

Recognize what is really going on.

Your child is being chosen as a subject for a massive, unprecedented experiment using powerful mood-altering drugs to modify the behavior of young people. It is vitally important that you know and understand the following concepts.

I. Selection

Your child is being selected out because of "unacceptable" behavior. Institutional psychiatry and compulsory, age-graded, competitive education have many things in common. For one, both place a high value on SELEC-TION. You need to recognize that your child, along with hundreds of thousands of other youngsters, is being selected out based on a judgment that his or her behavior is unacceptable. Psychiatry and education bear the burden of a societal mandate to enforce sameness and conformity as evidenced by proper adjustment to institutional standards. There is precious little room for celebrating uniqueness and diversity.

II. Selection means diagnosis means treatment.

You need to recognize the illusion that underlies the entire process of labeling and diagnosing children. Your child is selected, and you are referred to a "mental health professional" (a medical doctor psychiatrist or a university doctor psychologist) for an "evaluation" to determine a "diagnosis" and decide whether your child really does have a psychiatric disorder. The truth is that the whole process of psychiatric evaluation and diagnosis is, for the most part, a sham.[2] Once your child is selected, a thoroughly predictable process with thoroughly predictable results is set in motion. It is extremely rare for a child referred to a psychiatrist or psychologist for evaluation of a "disruptive behavior disorder" (DBD) not to be given a diagnosis. These people are in the business of giving diagnoses. And DBDs (including conduct disorders and so-called ADHD) *are one of those peculiar "diseases" in which the subjective experience of the adults around the*

---

[2] There may at times be value in educational diagnosis if it is done by someone who really knows and understands how children learn. All too often professionals have little awareness of the absurdity of age-segregated learning and the expectation that all children should learn at the same pace in the same style.

"patient" determine the presence of the "disease." The main criteria for diagnosis have nothing to do with the state of the "patient's" body or psyche.

Furthermore, you need to know that diagnosis is not really about describing your child in a way that will give useful information to help enhance development. *Psychiatric diagnosis is not descriptive, but prescriptive.* Just as referral almost inevitably leads to diagnosis, diagnosis means treatment. When your child is selected out as a behavior problem, he or she is being chosen for "treatment" and "special" services.

III. Treatment means drugs.

You need to know that institutional psychiatry operates from a narrow viewpoint called BioPsychiatry, which is based on three specific assumptions.

The first assumption is that human distress is a result of "mental illness." The second is that "mental illness" consists of a tremendous (and growing all the time) assortment of "diseases" classified together in the psychiatric bible: the Diagnostic and Statistical Manual (DSM) of the American Psychiatric Association. By translating human behavior into medical diseases, this manual acts as a key to open the treasure chest of medical health insurance dollars. Incredibly enough, problems with school behavior have been translated into this system. "Treatment" of these disorders is now an extremely profitable and rapidly growing business for the pharmacology industry and psychiatric profession. The third assumption of BioPsychiatry, then, is that these "diseases" are caused by biological and genetic defects in the "sick" individual. The "treatment" of choice for your poor child is, of course, pharmacological (i.e., drugs).

IV. These drugs are dangerous.

You are told that these drugs are benign. You need to recognize that this is self-serving misinformation. I will only mention Ritalin, which is by far most popular; an estimated 2,000,000 young people, mostly boys, are on this drug. You probably were not told that Ritalin is "speed," pharmacologically classified with amphetamines and having the same effects, side effects and risks. The FDA classifies Ritalin in a high addictive category (Schedule II) along with amphetamines, cocaine, morphine, opium, and barbiturates. This drug's adverse reactions are described below, in an excerpt from the *Physicians Desk Reference* (PDR) on the potential adverse reactions caused by Ritalin:

> Nervousness and insomnia are the most common adverse reactions but are usually controlled by reducing dosage and omitting the drug in the afternoon and the evening. Other reactions include hypersensitivity (including skin rash), urticaria [swollen, itching patches of skin], fever, arthralgia, exfoliative dermatitis [scaly patches of skin], erythema multiforme [an acute inflammatory skin disease], with histopathological findings of necrotizing vasculitis [destruction of the blood vessels], and thrombocytopenic purpura [a serious blood clotting disorder]; anorexia; nausea; dizziness; palpitations; headache; dyskinesia [impairment of voluntary muscle movement]; drowsiness; blood pressure and pulse changes, both up and down; tachycardia [rapid heartbeat]; angina [spasmodic attacks of intense heart pain]; cardiac arrhythmia [irregular heartbeat]; abdominal pain, weight loss during prolonged therapy.

There have been rare reports of Tourette's syndrome. Toxic psychosis has been reported in patients taking this drug; luekopenia [reduction in white blood cells] and/or anemia; a few instances of scalp hair loss. In children, loss of appetite, abdominal pain, weight loss during prolonged therapy, insomnia, and tachycardia may occur more frequently; however, any of the other adverse reactions listed above may also occur.

Robert Mendelsohn, M.D., a well-known and outspoken critic of much standard medical practice comments on the above excerpt:

This is the kind of information about a drug that the manufacturer is compelled by law to share with the doctors who will prescribe it. Unfortunately, there is no law requiring that the doctors who prescribe the drug share the information about its potentially damaging or fatal effects with you. That is why I have provided so much information about Ritalin, which applies, as well, to its counterparts. (1984, pp. 203-4)

It should also be mentioned that Ritalin stunts the growth of the child's whole body including the brain. This is one reason "drug holidays" (periods of time off from taking the drug) tend to be emphasized. More subtle, but profound, is the arrest of emotional and social development. Children are denied the opportunity to work through issues and the maturation process drug free. Finally, I think there is a significant tendency of child Ritalin users to become addicted to psychiatric (or street) drugs well into their adolescent years and longer. I haven't seen research studies on this, but I have seen a great deal of anecdotal evidence.

The Austin TV news reported last year that Ritalin was the most popular recreational drug on the University of Texas campus. After conducting an eight-month investigation, John Merrow, executive producer of a public television documentary on ADHD, in an Op-ed piece published in *The New York Times,* October 21, 1995, reported:

> Ritalin is so plentiful that in some junior high schools it's a "gateway drug," the first drug a child experiments with. "I used to mix it with marijuana," a recovering teenage addict in Maryland said. "It gives you a nice buzz." Reports of Ritalin theft and abuse in schools are commonplace, alarming the Drug Enforcement Agency (DEA). "We've now begun to see deaths from this drug," said Mr. Haislip, DEA Director of Diversion Control. "We had a recent death in Roanoke, where a child died from snorting this drug like Cocaine."

Merrow also reported that Ritalin's manufacturer, Ciba-Geigy, has given nearly $900,000 in cash grants to a group called Children and Adults with Attention Deficit Disorder (CHADD). This money, along with in-kind services, has helped CHADD grow from a small regional organization into a national powerhouse with 35,000 members, 650 chapters and clout in Washington. CHADD is lobbying to relax DEA controls on Ritalin. In the meantime, the propaganda is relentless.

V. These drugs do not help your child.

You are told that Ritalin really works, that it has been proven effective. What this means is that some children "behave much better" when they're on Ritalin. Proponents of the drug will tell you that the drug works because it corrects a biological/neurological defect in the child. You need to know that this is entirely a statement of faith on the order of a religious belief. There is no scientific evidence to show any consistent biological or genetic cause of any problem routinely seen by psychiatrists, most definitely including the so-called DBDs of school children. Children diagnosed as ADHD do not respond to Ritalin because it corrects a biological defect; they respond because they're taking an amphetamine. A long-demonstrated effect of amphetamines is that users experience a narrowed focus of attention and concentration on detail and are less in touch with their real feelings. Any child becomes more docile, obedient and willing to concentrate on boring, repetitive tasks—all desirable qualities in a school setting.

You need to know also that Ritalin is addictive, that it interferes with development (including that of the brain) and that many children experience other serious effects, including permanent disfiguring tics. As a stimulant, Ritalin can cause the very things it is supposed to cure—inattention, hyperactivity and aggression. Withdrawal effects, such as the child getting upset after missing a single dose, are *mistakenly* interpreted as a sign that the child needs to be put back on medication. What they probably *didn't* tell you is that "years of research and clinical use have failed to confirm any positive long-term effects from Ritalin in behavior or academic performance." (Breggin & Breggin, p. 84)

VI. Recognize Adultism.

Adultism is the systematic mistreatment of children and young people simply because they are young. The overall conditioning against emotional expression is laid down through adultism. The pattern is one of massive disrespect. To test whether or not you are acting as an agent of this oppression, apply the following question to any action you take toward a young person: *Would you treat another adult the same way?* Since we are all thoroughly conditioned to treat children a certain way, we must make every effort to challenge our conditioning.

VII. Recognize the code word "Potential."

The use of the word "potential" is all too reflective of a corporate economic emphasis on future profit. Focusing on a child's "potential" is subtle adultism, and adults who do so have lost sight of the child. *Do not trust the thinking of anyone who keeps emphasizing the "potential" of your child;* rather, put your trust in those who can celebrate and delight in who your child already is. It is good to have *relaxed,* high expectations for your child. Just don't let your expectations distract you from paying attention to what is going on now. I think it is probably most wise and accurate to assume that *whatever your child is doing now,* whatever she is showing you now, *is already a brilliant expression of what she needs now.* It's our challenge as parents or other adult allies to think well and respond effectively.

I was at an extended family gathering with my then almost 5-year-old daughter. Vanessa showed a picture she had just created to her great aunt. Aunt Helen responded lovingly, saying to Vanessa, "What a great artist you are going to be when you grow up!" I think my daughter's response reveals the essence of what I'm trying to say here. Vanessa was insulted. She boldly faced my aunt, with hands on hips, and declared, "I already am!"

Summary

The bottom line is to recognize that you are being expected to unquestioningly accept a decision for your child that she be selected out for special treatment and given drugs. You are expected to believe that your child has a disease and that this special treatment is for his own good. You are often made to question your own responsibility and worth as a parent if you choose to resist something that is so obviously necessary and good for your "special" child. The reality, as you can see, is very different than this Alice-in-Wonderland, upside-down distortion.

CHAPTER 2
About Schools

The Thing About School

Later in this book, I have a lot to say about the individual child—ways to think about problems with mood, behavior, attention and concentration, ways to help a child in these areas. The point I am really emphasizing just now, however, is that it is dangerous and harmful to reduce the dynamic interactional phenomena of our society's interface with young people to the biological psychopathology of children. Children have a hard time when their needs are not well met, when we have failed in our moral imperative to provide an excellent atmosphere for them to grow and develop. As the focus of this book is what to do when your child is labeled a problem by the schools, it is important to give thought to schools in our society.

The nature of oppression is to make us forget. John Taylor Gatto, New York City Teacher of the Year for two years running, has unearthed and made public the history and philosophical underpinnings of our system of education. Have you ever wondered how and why it is that we do education the way we do: compulsory attendance; rigidly defined curricula; age segregation; single adult authority; brief class periods with rigid, frequent transitions; etc.? Have you thought a lot about what development goals the designers of such a system had in mind?

Much was written in the late 1960s and early 1970s decrying the deleterious effects of our compulsory education system. Writers such as John Holt, Paul Goodman and Jonathan Kozol detailed the damage our system does to young people. They saw how this system was based on a factory model that promoted efficiency and productivity as the primary values. The system was needed to engineer a massive psychic shift from independent, land-based people to dependent town people reliant on jobs offered by the captains of industry. Gatto's research shows how we adopted a Prussian model that was developed and proved effective for the intention of creating obedient soldiers and loyalists for the State. Leading thinkers who developed the philosophy of the United States system of compulsory education were, for the most part, trained in Germany. Gatto quoted the theoretical writings of these men. They were very clear that the function of education was to instill primary values of obedience and acquiescence to authority. In order to do so, the system was designed to enforce utter dependency and discourage original, independent thought. In short, according to Gatto, the idea was to foster "alienation from the individual's own soul."

In retrospect and in the light of rhetoric praising independence and creativity, the words of these men seem appalling. The fact is, however, that our system continues to operate on these principles and the results continue to be devastating. Gatto's 1992 book, *Dumbing Us Down,* clearly describes primary effects of this type of education. He describes our schools as inherently *psychopathic;* rigid and systematic and constant interruption of young people's self-directed work at 45-minute intervals shows a total lack of conscience, sensitivity, awareness, and respect for the natural desires, inclinations and tendencies of unique individuals.

The subtitle of Gatto's book, *"The Hidden Curriculum of Compulsory Schooling,"* refers to seven lessons that he contends are taught from Harlem to Hollywood Hills:

1. **Confusion** - Everything is out of context with constant violations of natural order and sequence. While it is the nature of human beings to seek meaning and relatedness, what students get is disconnected facts and the unrelatedness of everything.
2. **Class Position** - Students stay in the class where they belong, in good order, with their own kind.
3. **Indifference** - The lesson of bells is that no work is worth finishing, so why care too deeply about anything.
4. **Emotional Dependency** - A comprehensive system of rewards and punishments enforces dependency and teaches children to surrender their will.
5. **Intellectual Dependency** - The belief that good students wait for a teacher to tell them what to do says it all and is taught early on in our system. Success means doing assigned thinking, limiting ideas to received thought, sacrificing original and independent thinking.
6. **Provisional Self-Esteem** - Students are constantly evaluated and judged. Individual worth is not inherent, but clearly and constantly contingent on the evaluations of certified professionals.
7. **One Can't Hide** - Students are not allowed private spaces or private time; homework extends the system's surveillance right into private homes.

No one is unaffected by this process. It is important to understand that it is not the content that is really the problem; alterations of content don't make a lot of difference. It is the method that is inexorable. As Gatto concludes, "School is a 12-year jail sentence where bad habits are the only curriculum truly learned." It is no wonder that most of us carry massive self-doubt and have tremendous difficulty thinking independently and challenging authority.

Another factor contributing to this problem of crushed creativity and original thinking is *propaganda*. Leonard Frank (1995) includes a wonderful quotation from Aldous Huxley regarding what happened to a movement at the advent of World War II intended to facilitate critical thinking and what he called "Propaganda Analysis."

> Certain educators disapproved of the tracking of propaganda analysis on the grounds that it would make adolescents unduly cynical. Nor was it welcomed by the military authorities, who were afraid that recruits might start to analyze the utterances of drill sergeants. And then there were the clergymen and advertisers. The clergymen were against propaganda analysis as tending to undermine belief and diminish churchgoing; the advertisers objected on the grounds that it might undermine brand loyalty and reduce sales. (On the Institute for Propaganda Analysis, which was founded in the United States in 1937 and folded in 1941, "Education for Freedom.")

It is instructive to combine Gatto's concept of the modern "psychopathic" school with the BioPsychiatric concept of individual "psychopathology." I suggest the following conclusions as more valid than those of BioPsychiatry:

- Psychopathology does *not* cause children to fail.
- Psychopathic schools, having no conscience and insensitive to the needs and motivations of children, are a failure to children.

What we call childhood psychopathology (e.g., ADHD) is a result. "Disruptive Behavior Disorders" are a distorted way of describing the effect, not the cause, of a bankrupt philosophy of education.

Schools and Shame

A basic reality about schools is that the vast majority of young people have no choice about attendance. Home schooling is growing in this country, but for most families it is not an option; the same is true for other alternative modes of schooling. It is vitally important that parents find ways to protect children from the negative effects of our current education system. When Gatto was speaking in Austin, Texas, an audience member asked him what could be done to help a child who had to go to a traditional school. I will paraphrase Gatto's response, as his view is very much like my own.

The thing about schools as we know them is that they are *guaranteed* to violate a child's natural instinct for curious, zestful, self-directed learning. *The inherently psychopathic structure and scheduling* of our schools, dictated by an industrially ordered adult society, cannot help but clash with a child's natural needs, inclinations and interests. Therefore, *it is absolutely inevitable that somebody has to be wrong.* That *somebody* is either the child or the school (and its representatives such as teacher, coach, or principal). We are not applying the word *"wrong"* in the sense of making a mistake; the issue goes much deeper than that. We are saying that either the child or the school is fundamentally flawed. Given the enormous disparity in power, and children's natural tendency to experience themselves as responsible centers of the universe, unprotected children will inevitably assume that they are defective for not fitting in.

This unfortunate sense of self is often referred to as poor self-esteem. The emotional concept that one is fundamentally flawed or defective is called SHAME. It is an awful feeling. It makes one want to hide because it feels unbearable to be exposed. You hide. You don't speak out. You worry what others think. You feel miserable.

Boredom

There are many factors that contribute to children's experience of school-related shame, including Gatto's seven lessons outlined above and the overall disruption of self-directed learning. I want to emphasize boredom now because I think we tend to underestimate just how stressful and suppressive boredom can be. In so doing, I am well aware of an apparent contradiction in this book, since I later challenge the demand for constant stimulation and entertainment. I argue that we need to slow life down for our children, to allow relaxed, quiet time and time in nature. I discuss the concept of "down time" as a necessary condition of withdrawal from overstimulation and as a space for incubation of creative expression. Here I present an opposite face, arguing that we need to stimulate and challenge our children; both are true. It is said in Buddhist tradition that the guardians of truth are paradox and confusion. So it appears with questions of time and activity.

I came across a passage recently from the autobiography of Jacques Lusseyran, a man blinded in an accident at age 8 who as a teenager was a key leader of the underground French resistance to Nazi Germany in World War II. Lusseyran's story is amazing. At the same time that he was leading the resistance work, he studied an intense curriculum at the French lycèe, or preparatory school. What follows are the words of Lusseyran:

> I have already said that for blind people there
> is such a thing as moral odor, and I think that was
> the case at school. A group of human beings who

stay in one room by compulsion — or because of social obligation which comes to the same thing — begins to smell. That is literally the case, and with children it happens even faster. Just think how much suppressed anger, humiliated independence, frustrated vagrancy and impotent curiosity can be accumulated by forty boys between the ages of ten and fourteen!

So that was the source of the unpleasant odor and the smoke which, for me, was like a physical presence in class. What I saw there was confusion, colors were faded and even dirty. The blackboard was black, the floor was black, the tables were black and so were the books. Even the teacher, in terms of light, was no more than gray. To be otherwise he had to be remarkable, not only for what he knew (learning in those days gave me little light) but remarkable as a person as well.

Boredom bound and gagged all my senses. Even sounds in class lost their volume and their depth and went lifeless. *Every bit of my passion for living was needed to stand the test.* At bottom I must have lacked discipline, not making up my mind to rebel, but still an incorrigible individualist. That was certainly part of my make-up, but then too there was blindness and its special world, to which school was doing violence. *I had to wait years,* at least until adolescence, *to quiet the scandal which started inside my head at school.* I doubt whether I have made peace with it even now.

As for the subject of all subjects, the fact that the world is not just outside us but also within, this was entirely lacking. I understood that the teacher could not or did not wish to talk about what was going on inside him. That was his affair, and after all I was not anxious myself to talk about what went on in me. But the inner life was so much more than a personal thing. There were a thousand desires and goals my companions shared with me, and I knew it. To accumulate knowledge was good and beautiful, but the reason for men to acquire it would have been more meaningful, and no one spoke of that.

I could not help thinking that in the whole business someone was cheating somewhere. I felt I had to defend myself, and I did so by mobilizing all the images of my inner world, all the ones bound up with living creatures or living things. Sitting on my dark chair in front of my sickening table, under the gray downpour of learning, I set myself to weaving a kind of cocoon. Still, while I was a good boy I was sly, and managed it so that no one would guess I was hostile. This interior world of mine was so important to me that I was determined to protect it from shipwreck, and to rescue it I never stopped making concessions to the public, to books, to my parents and teachers. I owe my brilliance as a student to this rescue operation.

In order to be left in peace I undertook to learn everything they wanted me to, Latin, entomology, geometry and the history of the Chaldeans. I learned to type on an ordinary typewriter so I could hand my homework directly to the teachers like the others. Every day I carried my Braille typewriter to school, and put it on a felt cushion to deaden the sound, and then I took my notes. I listened, responded, listened, but was never in it heart and soul. As a boy I was cut in two. I was there and elsewhere, always going and coming between the important and the meaningless.

Now that the experience is behind me — the boredom thick as oil, the moral curvature which lasted for years — I can see that I owe them something, as the sign that *some vital spirit in me refused to turn its back on childhood,* and would never admit that truth was ready-made. There was no going back on it. I would never relinquish the sense of wonder I felt when I went blind. Even if there were not a book in the world to record it, I should still feel it. (1963, pp. 65 - 68.) (italics mine)

Boredom can be extremely stressful; every bit of Lusseyran's passion was needed "to stand the test." So many of our schools today teach to the test, to state exams measuring academic achievement. Boredom can be deadening; all Lusseyran's senses were "bound and gagged" by boredom. He could not help but think that "someone was cheating somewhere;" this is the violation that leads to shame. "Some vital spirit" in Lusseyran prevailed, after he "had to wait years to quit the scandal that started inside my head at school." Even looking back as a university professor writing his autobiography, Lusseyran doubts he had made peace with it. Hopefully your child's school is more humane than the French lycée; I don't know. I am sure, however, that the eloquent words of this brilliant blind man are still relevant. I hope they inspire you to think well and help protect your child from shame.

The following dialogue is intended to assist you toward this end.

A Little Dialogue About Handling School Shame

PARENT So, what can a parent do to give a child some protection from taking on this shame?

JOHN Well, it's really tricky. What makes it tricky is that your child has to go to school and you don't want to spoil it for your child by judging and condemning the people and place where you are sending her to grow and develop. You want your child to do well, enjoy learning, have excellent relationships with caring teachers, and be happy about getting up in the morning to go to school. Furthermore, you don't want to torment yourself with feelings of dread and guilt over this awful thing you are forcing on your child.

PARENT So, come on already, what can a parent do?

JOHN Well, it's really tricky. What makes it tricky is that you don't want to spoil it for your child by making him into a victim. Yes, it is tricky, but you have an extremely fortunate piece of information on your side that is rock-solid. *You and your child are extremely intelligent and completely capable of handling the greatest of challenges. With good information and good support, together you can handle just about anything really well; that most definitely includes the challenge of school.*

PARENT All right already, would you please get to the point. What can I do?

JOHN Bear with me. One more tricky part. I detect a little tension here; it's a good creative tension; *carpe* *diem.* Let's seize the day and use this tension to bring to life the challenging task of teaching independence and responsibility. What's tricky is that you want to help your child *and* you want to foster your child's independent handling of school as his responsibility. Just on that edge of tension in "All right already, what can *I* do?" is a great place to be, right on the dynamic edge of those perilous illusions to which we fall prey in struggling with independence and responsibility. Too much support? (Doing it for your child?) Too little support? (Abandoning your child on an unequal playing field?) Unresolved guilt? (Am I forcing my poor baby to participate in an abusive situation?)

A key point to remember is that you need support to process these tense feelings. You're doing a great job and you deserve support. The attitude to reach for and embrace is one of *relaxed confidence,* for yourself and for your child. Once again, the absolute truth is that your child is completely intelligent and capable of handling life's challenges—with your best thinking, support, encouragement and active involvement as ally.

PARENT OK, but you still haven't told me what I can do to protect my child from shame.

JOHN My apologies for going on and on. The biggest thing, really, is that there *is* no formula. The greatest wisdom, and perhaps the greatest contradiction to our educational heritage of the received thought of others, is that you really can TRUST YOUR OWN THINKING. Get support for thinking out loud as you figure it out, and know that your child and your situation are unique.

Beyond this, here is Gatto's point. What you need to do is to give your child a buffer or shield for protection against personally taking on the inevitable failures of school to support her inherent nature and self-directed learning. What you need to do is to figure out a way to let your child know that *yes, there is something wrong, but not with you!*

I hope you understand why I needed such a lengthy preamble to this deceptively simple advice. Your child needs to know that there are problems with how schooling is done; that his or her feelings are understandable; that it's regrettable we don't have a better alternative; that it's not the child's fault. To have such an enlightened witness can make all the difference for a child and prevent the shame from penetrating quite as deeply into a child's core.

To communicate this well requires great creativity and flexibility in thinking. It requires being sensitive to children's thinking and development; it is important to give information according to *their* need, not your own. Your judgments about the school may not correlate very well with your child's experience.

Most important is that feeling attitude of relaxed confidence! Your child is great. She'll do well. Together, you'll handle whatever comes up, whatever it takes. Mistakes are OK. Children don't need perfect parents. Your child needs a really good, involved, imperfect parent. You're the one.

CHAPTER 3
An Alternative 3 Rs

Tammy Cox, director of *The Redirection Connection* in Austin, Texas, proposed these alternative 3 Rs: Respect, Responsibility and Relationship. A woman of great spirit and thought, Tammy's mission is to educate adults in the ways of democratic, respectful parenting and child-raising. I believe that a clear understanding of these three concepts helps ensure a rich and successful experience as adults and young people grow together. What follows is my attempt to help create this clear understanding and attitude.

Respect

Complete and unqualified respect is and must be the foundation stone of any mutually satisfying relationship, and must be the basis from which we enter into relationships with our children. Without it, we all inevitably end up in humiliation and disgrace. As I said above, the pattern of adultism is one of massive disrespect.

I think adultism — treating young people with less than complete respect—is grounded in a fundamental distortion in how we see and experience the nature of the world and especially the nature of human beings. In the following sections (especially that on relationship), I have included suggestions to help you correct this distorted perception. For now, it is enough to say that we carry a heavy load of shame about our nature and a horrible wound from being torn apart from our naturally complete interconnectedness with all of life. The sum total of our experience has resulted in an awful misunderstanding about the nature of being human. Incredibly, we are pulled to view our children as inherently lazy, irresponsible, stupid and manipulative in the worst sense of these words. So we justify disrespectful attempts to control or punish them as necessary to shape them properly or correct their brutish, natural tendencies; all this is done "for their own good," of course.

Children are already completely good, just as, by nature, are you. All of us are born good, always have been good, and are good now. Anything else is a *result* of having been hurt.

You will see in the next section on responsibility that I do not equate permissiveness with respect. It is useful to view children as coming into the world with great intelligence, but with equally great lack of information and experience in the ways of the world. Furthermore, there is an obvious, dramatic inequity in size and power. So being a parent is a *tremendous* responsibility, and we need all the help we can get. Developing is a *tremendous* challenge for young people. They need all the help we can provide — thoughtful, well-considered help, tempered by a good understanding of human nature and development.

Just now, I want to offer four suggestions in thinking about respect. First and foremost, always remember that your child, however small and dependent, however emotionally vehement about his frustrating and helpless condition, is not only what he appears to be as a little, needy, emotional human animal. She is, in essence, a vast spiritual being undergoing the immensely challenging task of learning to live and master the ways of being in a physical body in this physical world. I offer the wisdom of Kahlil Gibran, from *The Prophet,* as a reminder:

And a woman who held a babe against her
   bosom said, Speak to us of Children.
And he said:
Your children are not your children.
They are the sons and daughters of Life's long-
   ing for itself.
They come through you but not from you,
And though they are with you yet they belong
   not to you.
You may give them your love but not your
   thoughts,
For their souls dwell in the house of tomorrow,
   which you cannot visit, not even in your
   dreams.
You may strive to be like them, but seek not to
   make them like you.
For life goes not backward nor tarries with yes-
   terday.
You are the bows from which your children as
   living arrows are sent forth.
The archer sees the mark upon the path of the
   infinite, and He bends you with His might
   that His arrows may go swift and far.
Let your bending in the Archer's hand be for
   gladness;
For even as He loves the arrow that flies, so He
   loves also the bow that is stable.

Let's replace adultism with awe.

My next three suggestions form a set of interrelated
basic teachings about respect. A frequent complaint of
parents, and one which we all experience at times and to
varying degrees, is that, in Rodney Daingerfield's famous
trademark, "We Get No Respect!" "My child is impolite,

rude, disrespectful, etc. to me! He better learn respect." "If she expects me to treat her with respect, she's going to have to show me some respect." This ubiquitous phenomenon offers a great focal point for clarification about respect and parenting.

The second teaching I offer is this: *The way to teach respect is to give it.* The *only* way your child will learn the true meaning and experience of respect is through being consistently treated with respect. Please know here that the type of learning to which I refer is not a disembodied, conceptual-intellectual knowledge; it is a learning at the core of one's beingness about respect as the natural order of one's inner and outer worlds. *Our job as parents specifically, and as human beings in general, is to do* **whatever it takes** *to heal and release our cynicism and move into a place of Sacred Respect for ourselves, our children, our world.*

The next teaching follows naturally. It is the nature of human beings that we come into the world expecting (experienced parents know that "demanding" is a more appropriate word here!) to be treated with complete respect. Anything less naturally evokes outrage and indignation. Imagine a 2-year-old child standing in the middle of your living room with a glass of juice. You notice her and she spills some on your newly cleaned, beautiful rug. Without even thinking, you naturally react; words come out of your mouth something like "Daughter, you know better!" or worse, or simply "Daughter!" Difficult to convey on paper, but essential to my point here, is that the words *per se* are less important than the tone and energy of your voice. Think about it and you will know whether there was an edge, or more than an edge, of shame (accusatory judgment, disgust, *disrespect)* in your reaction.

What's interesting is this. A child who has already been sufficiently cowed by fear and shame may very well respond timidly and fearfully to your reaction, perhaps obeying and moving off the rug, perhaps dropping the glass in startled fear. A child who has not been shamed, however, will very likely respond something like this. Imagine that two-year-old again. She hears your voice and her body naturally reacts with a startle. She does not cow and comply, however. Rather, she regains her composure and looks at you defiantly. Then, looking you right in the eye, she ceremoniously pours out the rest of the juice on your precious rug!

Raising a child to be proud and to know his inherent worth often does not make parenting easy. In fact, it seems to force an ongoing process of humble acknowledgment and working through of the places we've been hurt, where we carry shame and are overcome by patterns of disrespect.

Tammy Cox summarized this particular teaching for me in these words: *It is more important for your child to defy and resist disrespectful efforts to control him than it is to have things work well in his life.* Self-respect and autonomy are very high priorities in the order of your child's existence; order and flow in worldly affairs are most definitely a notch lower in the hierarchy of needs. Understanding this point will go a *long* way in understanding your experience as a parent. It also explains a great deal about young people's so-called "rebellion" in our society.

It may feel like a sad truth, but that sadness is really a grief carried over many years from the ways we were suppressed as children. The truth is that our young people's resistance is cause for celebration. *We cannot control our children, but they will respond well to our respect.* With respect as the basis of our relationship, they may at times accept, and at the very least consider, our stumbling efforts to provide them with loving guidance.

The final teaching I offer here goes deep into the heart of that often anguishing phenomenon of being treated "badly" by our children. I choose the word "badly" and put it in quotes to bring attention. "Bad" needs to be seen clearly for what it is: a judgment in the language of shame. Such a judgment has only negative value as a motivator for responsive parenting; it can only bring trouble in our relationships with our children. It is useful only as a signal to activate our own "shame sirens" and help us work on healing our own shame.

Your child is not bad. She is showing you something — a place where it is hard and she needs to work. And do you know what? As so often is the case, it is very likely true that things are not even close to what they appear to be. A great teacher of mine emphasized over and again that things are *fundamentally* upside down and backwards in the outer world. Whether this makes sense to you or not, whether you believe it or not, it is worth considering in various situations that are presented in everyday life. In the case of your disrespectful child, I am suggesting that much of the time, bad does indeed mean good! Let me explain.

The core of this teaching is about SAFETY. We are inevitably hurt as we go about living in this world. Children are inevitably hurt (treated with disrespect, rejected, frustrated, made to do things they don't want to do, etc.) as they go about their lives. Fortunately, we humans have a built-in mechanism for healing from these hurts that has to do with emotional expression. The hurts do not just go away; they must be healed and released by expression. And guess what? Safety is required for that expression to take place. Children are extremely intelligent; they quickly learn to suppress their expression if it is going to lead to greater hurts.

So who is the most likely candidate for safest person in a child's life? You are. That disrespectful "bad" behavior is very often a child's attempt to, in effect, use you as a counselor. Their "bad" behavior, then, may best be interpreted as a wonderful acknowledgment that you are a safe haven for them to show where they're having difficulty, release their frustrations and discharge their rejections by acting this out on you. It feels like hell at times, but it really is an honor. God knows we all need a lot of help with it, but it is a great gift you give your child. By allowing her to use you as a counselor this way, you are helping your child enjoy the world outside your home. How many of you have shaken your heads in wonder at another adult's comments (especially during a time when your child is challenging you big-time at home) about how wonderful, thoughtful, considerate, mature and well-behaved your child was in their presence? Amazing.

Responsibility

The first key in thinking about responsibility is to remember that children are inherently responsible. Young people naturally view themselves as the center of the universe and assume that whatever happens is because of them. This is why, beyond any direct attributions by the perpetrator, an abused child feels guilty and blames himself for the abuse. Bad things happen to me; therefore I must *be* bad. A view of children as inherently irresponsible and needing to be taught responsibility is dangerous;

adult perceptions and expectations exert a powerful influence on young people's self-image and behavior. Children don't need to be trained to be responsible, but they do need information and guidance, opportunity and encouragement.

The second key is based on the simple truth that what you do far outweighs what you say. As the old proverb goes, "Actions Speak Louder Than Words"; the best way to teach your child responsibility is to be responsible. As you model responsibility, you provide a family environment in which your child will thrive.

The third key is this: You teach a child responsibility by giving him responsibility. Better said, a young person learns to express her inherent natural responsibility in this world by being given responsibility. A trust is given, an expectation is conveyed, encouragements are ever-present, support and understanding are available when the going gets hard and frustrating.

Not only is it our inherent nature to be responsible, but it truly spoils us to be denied the opportunity to develop and express this gift. L. Ron Hubbard, father of Dianetics, proposes that natural law involves energy exchange. You can't really just give something away; you can't really just take something. To attempt to do so corrupts our nature, inducing false pride in the giver and false entitlement in the taker.

It seems to me that this is one law that provides a particularly challenging experience for parents. I maintain that the parent-child relationship is unique because, in many respects—economically, structurally, and emotionally—it is truly one-way.

This unique relationship between parents and children is natural and inevitable. Human beings require a long period of absolute dependency; failure to provide for this results in the kinds of lifelong dependency so pervasive in our society today. However, it is our job as parents to recognize that our children need and want responsibility and to provide experiences and support appropriate to their age level and maturity to help them master the ways of this world. My friend Donna Goertz referred to this learning as a spiritual incubation period, a natural extension of physical incubation in the womb.

I confess that my thinking about responsibility has been confused. As most people, I had learned to view responsibility as a burden, a pressure, a dreadful obligation. This has colored my experience as a parent. As a result, all too often I have seen my family through the eyes of resentment rather than the glorious "Eyes of Delight." In so doing, I have missed out on the daily gifts my children offer. My challenge now, and I extend this challenge to all of you, is to fully embrace my role as a parent, not as an obligation, but as one of the greatest opportunities and contributions a man can make. I give to my children with open heart. I take delight in their presence. I willingly sacrifice. I allow myself to be imperfect, and I get support from others during my inevitable emotional upheavals. I know what an incredibly hard job parenting is, *and maybe some day I'll get some rest!*

One word of caution to parents: We get stuck in our attempts to parent well in places where we have "frozen needs" (unmet dependency needs from our own childhoods). We are unconsciously pulled to look to our children to help us heal from the hurts of these unmet needs. However, our responsibility as adults is to seek counseling and support elsewhere. *Do not* expect your children to meet *your* emotional needs; your job is to meet *theirs*.

Relationship

Respect, responsibility and relationship are all inter-related. Respect is the foundation of all relationship, and responsibility is the ongoing action that maintains the relationship. Throughout this book I emphasize the personal relationship between parent and child. I am aware that I do not address what we usually refer to as our "relationship," our primary significant other. I know how profoundly children are affected by the quality of their parents' relationship. We must, married or not, do everything within our power to make this good, to be loving and cooperative co-parents for our children. In this section, however, I urge you to glimpse the bigger picture of your child's life. Our children have and need us as parents, but they also have extended families and friends, communities of people, plants, animals, the waters, the air, the trees, the earth and sky. It is our job as parents to hold a big enough space for all of this in our children's development and to help them be in relationship with all these forms of life and with the spirit which sustains us all.

In order to most effectively help our young people, we must get really clear about where we stand, which, in our modern world, feels like extremely shaky ground. The fundamental root of our problem with relationship is that we are out of balance with the natural order of our existence. We are living in the midst of a shared delusion that I call "consensual madness." This means that we have created and allow ourselves to live in a world of massive disorder. Nuclear proliferation, war and famine, desertification and pollution and other forms of environmental degradation shape our daily lives. We inhabit a world in which masses of people live in decaying urban centers. Human beings are wonderfully loving, highly intelligent creatures. It is a great violation of the human spirit that we give toxic, mood-altering drugs to hundreds of thousands of our precious children. Things have to be seriously out of balance for this to occur.

Chellis Glendinning wrote a book recently with a powerfully evocative title, one that, if you allow, will resonate as truth inside your body: *My Name Is Chellis and I'm in Recovery from Western Civilization*. Her thesis, with which I obviously agree, is that simply by virtue of living in today's disjointed, alienated, frenetic society, we are all to some degree suffering from chronic post-traumatic stress. Most of us feel like the proverbial "strangers in a world we never made." It is difficult, when we feel so much like passive victims, to reclaim our power and our responsibility to act consciously for ourselves, for our children, and for our planet.

So how do we move toward a right experience of relationship? It is important to realize that any attempt to do so will unavoidably bring us face to face with the intense psychological conditioning that forms the basis of the disordered and imbalanced existence we see today. My clear conviction is that, as with any teaching we wish to offer our children, we must become the teaching (or at least be open to and involved in the process of becoming the teaching) in order to pass it on. We convey to our children who we are. A good beginning is to explore the conditioning that affects us so deeply.

Our Philosophical Soil

We can go back just a bit in history to the 16th Century time of the Inquisition and to the horrific torture and killing of women as witches. A guiding theology set body and nature apart from soul and attacked women as embodiments of sinful nature. The official cosmology can be briefly summarized. Heaven and the angels in perfection were at the distant perimeter. Human beings, flawed and fallen creatures, were at the bottom of the universe. Earth was the cesspool of creation; the lowest level was Hell, the center of the Earth. An image from Dante's *Divine Comedy* may be used to highlight the situation; the precise center of the universe and of Hell was Satan's anus, frozen forever. This is the soil out of which our environmental crisis has grown. Human beings are fallen sinners, guilty and ashamed.

The Harvest

Environmental degradation, ecological disasters, global warming, polluted air, fouled waters, overflows of toxic wastes, nuclear proliferation and radiation poisoning, pesticide and chemical intrusion at every level of our food chain, planet desertification, eradication of our rain forests, a shrinking biodiversity with daily extinction of species—the list goes on and on and is all too familiar. This is a huge share of the harvest grown from the ground of Dante's *Divine Comedy*. It is the fulfillment of a prophecy; it has become "the cesspool of creation."

The age of reason and its scientific revolution gradually replaced theology as our primary way of viewing the world. Unfortunately, this view led us to deny our animal nature. Judeo-Christian attitudes about humans and nature transferred very well to the new scientific paradigm. If anything, the insults of Copernicus, that Earth was not the center of the Universe, and of Darwin, that humans were not specially created, only provided fuel for the fire. As the age of Newton provided the possibility, American historian Theodore Roszak, in his book on

EcoPsychology, *The Voice of the Earth* (1992), persuasively argues that industrial progress could only and still can only foul the Earth since its guiding principles are so inherently mad. To quote Roszak, "The species that destroys its own habitat in pursuit of false values, in willful ignorance of what it does, is 'mad' if the word means anything." (p. 68) Restoration to sanity requires a radical reordering of the consensual madness.

I have already said much about the incredibly distorted world view of BioPsychiatry and its reduction of human beings to a soulless physio-chemical-mechanical existence. The history of psychology is also understandably skewed; how could it not be, given the philosophical soil out of which it grew? How could it not be, given the recent historical realities of the Industrial Revolution? I am laying groundwork here necessary for an effective response to the question of how to move toward a healthy experience of balance and order in relationship. I believe the growing development of what we call EcoPsychology is part of our answer.

The Heart of EcoPsychology

The heart of EcoPsychology involves a colossal re-ordering of our inherited understanding and experience of human nature. We began the recent history of Western society from a ground of Judeo-Christian theology in which human beings were shameful, fallen sinners living in the cesspool of creation. In this view, the only hope for clear, clean, saving energy was by a God who was "wholly other," separate from nature and separate from our own natural bodies. The age of scientific reason only transferred this core state of sin to a denatured objectivity; the technological revolution provided incredible means to feed this consensual delusion that we are separate from nature. The recent blips in our planet's history, which Roszak calls City Pox, are "declarations of wishful biological independence from the natural environment. . . the modern city. . . the ancient dream of a totally encapsulated existence free of disease, dependency, the dirt and discomfort of organic life, perhaps even finally of death" (Roszak, pp. 219-220). No wonder this is the result when reared on a vision that we are fallen sinners or mere accidents in a random mechanistic universe, "strangers and afraid in a world we never made."

Psychology developed in the context of a shift in worldview from theology to science, the main assumptions about human nature remaining intact. The task of socialization (formerly salvation) was to harness or tame or civilize the unruly forces of our inherently dangerous animalistic drives or instincts (fallen sinners in foul bodies). The best to hope for was adequate adjustment to consensual reality, which was not to be questioned. So human nature was fundamentally flawed (original sin).

More and more people today are beginning to realize the truth about human beings—that our nature is inherently good, innocent, caring, compassionate, intelligent and completely worthy. This is a great step for psychology, but it is still a long way from EcoPsychology. Psychology still has incredible difficulty seeing its way out of a huge and fundamental error. It is like the fish knowing the nature of its water. Modern psychological theory is and always has been an artifact of urban-industrial life. It was built on the premise of an autonomous psyche (soul), independent not only from its surroundings but from its own body. Some psychological theories have reclaimed the body. Others have gradually expanded a relational world to include first the mother, then others, but almost always only humans. With no place for non-human life, we live and develop apart from the natural world.

Roszak agrees that this is the fundamental error of psychology. This apartness is the essence of our consensual madness. Furthermore, as fish can do little about fouled water, psychotherapy in urban-industrial office buildings is inherently limited in its ability to restore human beings to their rightful minds. Roszak returns to his beloved Romantic poets for inspiration and to another poet, Thomas Traherne, who predated them by two generations:

> All mine! And seen so easily! How great, How
>   Blest!
> How soon am I of all possest!
> My Infancie no sooner Opes its Eyes,
> But Straight the Spacious Earth
> Abounds with Joy Peace Glory Mirth
> And being Wise,
> The very Skies,
> And Stars do mine becom; being all possest
> Even in that Way that is the Best! (p. 298)

The environment that matters most is not the one we construct for our children; it is the one given them by nature. EcoPsychology is grounded in the reality that human beings are not apart from nature by theological design or cosmic error. Nature contains us and, borrowing a Native American expression, each of us is born with a capacity to experience awe and wonder for "All my relations." Our task is to reclaim or redevelop this natural capacity and to protect and nurture its reality for our children. From this place flows an enduring and abundant spring of clear, clean motivation as we live in our natural state of connectedness, of caring, of compassion, of love and reverence, knowing beyond any doubt that all life is sacred.

It is undoubtedly true that, as parents, we must do our best to ensure that our children experience a relationship with us, their primary caregivers, that is nurturing, comforting, encouraging, affectionate, delightful, completely close, fully human in the best sense. Much of this book, and certainly most of parenting/child-rearing guidance, stresses the importance of the human bond between parent and child. We know its power and significance.

Chellis Glendinning and Roszak and the theory of EcoPsychology remind us, however, that it is not enough to be the best lover and provider for your children. In order to respond to the challenge of being pressured to drug your child for "ADHD," you must first recognize what is really going on with BioPsychiatry and education and drugging children. In order to guide your child into a healthy experience of relationship, it is necessary first to recognize what is really going on with modern urban-industrial existence, to see and accept and feel the truth of Chellis Glendinning's teaching that we are all suffering some degree of chronic post-traumatic stress by virtue of living in a world out of balance. We must recognize and feel and respond to the reality of being *torn apart from* our natural relationship of complete interdependence. We must recover from our family of origin childhood wounds and make progress in treating our children well and with great respect. We must also move into "Recovery From Western Civilization" and learn or re-learn a respect that knows that all life is sacred. As awkward as it may feel, we must strive to know and experience complete connectedness with the natural world. It is vitally important, and such a tremendous gift, to allow our children great amounts of uninterrupted time and space to be with, play with and live in the natural world. They need to experience and know that they are forever naturally and completely *a part of* life in all its forms. It requires great clarity, conviction, determination and strength to shield and protect our children from the relentless onslaught of mindless technological forces that corrupt and destroy this beauty.

CHAPTER 4
Remembrances as Keys to Parent Heaven

Remember to Relax

Let go of any sense of urgency and pressure. Such feelings stem from adult fear and the need to avoid even more disturbing feelings of guilt, inadequacy, and loss of control. These are adult responses that have nothing to do with your child.

Remember that *you have all the time in the world.* You are committed to and involved with your child for the long haul. Remember the big picture, even as you sometimes struggle to make it through one day at a time: You and your child, working it out together, forever.

Remember also that these Disruptive Behavior Disorders are "funny diseases." They often disappear at the end of a school day or a school year. Present with one teacher, they mysteriously go into remission with another teacher. You have many years to watch your child grow and change as he develops and matures.

Remember the True Nature of Your Child

Children are neither small adults nor untrained animals needing to be disciplined and shaped. They are young human beings with enormous dependency needs. Completely dependent on adults for survival and proper development, children need abiding protection, nurturance and encouragement. Remember that *the inherent nature of children is that they are exceedingly intelligent, zestful, loving, and cooperative.* Children are born with an expectation that caring adults will respond to their needs in a good, loving, thoughtful way. Please do not allow this trust to be violated!

Remember also, and remember well, that our nature is that *we are completely connected with all of life!* An ancient Chinese saying is that in plucking a blade of grass, one strokes the stars. The ecological concept is called interdependence. There is an absurdly simple way to refute our cultural notion of rugged independence, of pulling oneself up by one's own bootstraps, of not needing anybody or anything. Simply ask this person or yourself to stop breathing. There is no getting around the simple truth that in living we are inextricably and unavoidably interdependent with all of life. This is our true nature. To act as if it were different, to hold a vision of anything less than this profound and simple truth, is to violate our children's trust.

Remember to have great empathy for your child; she has taken on a tremendous task. The early years of learning to be in this body in this world are a profound challenge. Steven and Ondrea Levine, in their 1995 book, *Embracing The Beloved: Relationship as a Path of Awakening,* remind us of a saying in the Sufi tradition that "This is not a world of my making or even of my choosing, but this is the world into which I am born to find the Beloved." The Levines go on to say that:

> Few would choose this realm of impermanence and holding as a rest stop, but many have discovered its value as a classroom. Birth is our painful initiation into the often awkward realm of relationship and duality. Sliding sideways into whatever niche is available in the family matrix we attempt to fit our whole ghost into an ever-

shifting world of people and things, of liking and disliking, of gain and loss. Born into a realm where most have denied happiness, clinging to momentary enjoyment, we often wander hopelessly between pleasure and pain, at times unable to distinguish between the two. (pp. 109-110)

Have great compassion for yourself and for your child. We tend to think of ourselves as human beings seeking a spiritual experience. As usual, the truth seems to be opposite and upside down from the appearance of things. Jacquie Small passed on this teaching to me:

We are not human beings having a spiritual experience; rather, *we are spiritual beings having a human experience.*

Consider that this may be the true nature of your child. Parenting is a tough job. We need to keep the big picture in mind as we grapple with the endless details and challenges.

Remember the Importance of Movement and Physical Activity

Remember how important movement and physical activity is to your developing child. This is such an integral aspect of your child's true nature that it deserves a section of its own. Our bodies are meant to move; this is especially important with children. Physiological and neurological development requires incredibly high levels of physical activity, from the infant's need to be carried in arms to the baby's crawling, the toddler's exploring and all the way through our development. Preschoolers and early school age children need to move, a lot.

I personally recommend the martial arts as an activity for young people. My own children have benefitted enormously from participation in karate. When properly taught, karate provides a wonderfully integrative experience of mind, body and spirit. On the physical level, flexibility, agility and power are developed. Emotionally, self-confidence and a sense of mastery come forward. Mentally, students develop great focus and concentration. With a good teacher, values of self and other respect and support are thoroughy ingrained. I have been extremely fortunate to have Suzanne Pinette of Sun Dragon Dojo in Austin, Texas, as my children's teacher. She is a highly skilled black belt with great values. She not only provides my children excellent technical guidance, but she also promotes excellent values. Perhaps most important for my children, she makes it fun!

My strong advice is to avoid a martial arts environment where emphasis is placed on competition. Also, avoid any teacher who is into "discipline" of students. Generally, "discipline" is a code word that really means punishment. Making students do pushups or other tasks as punishment (for being silly or not doing something well or any reason) is not about discipline in the sense of self-regulation and commitment. It is about authoritarian control; humiliating and disrespectful, such "discipline" instills fear and shame in a child. Let there be respect, let there be mastery, and let there be play. Make sure that an abiding teaching involves consistent support and respect for all peers and teachers—all for one and one for all.

I believe that movement and physical activity are vastly more important than academic and "so-called" intellectual development for children in the 4 to 8-year-old age group. I say "so-called" intellectual development because I think it is absurd to correlate intellect with academics, to reduce the concept of intelligence to the "mental" domain of life. I really agree with Joseph Chilton Pearce, author of *The Magical Child,* that tasks involving abstract intellectual activity (the use of symbols as in academia) are meant to come in a bit later, after age 8 on the average, in terms of cognitive development. The task of 4 to 8-year-olds is to fully develop their relationships with their bodies, with the earth, with the natural world. Pearce describes the task as a transfer from the matrix of "Mother" to that of "Earth." We are meant to experience ourselves as fully connected to the natural world. This connection is established by long, uninterrupted experience of active physical interaction with the natural world. The alternative, so common in urban existence as to be the norm, is to go through life feeling like we don't belong in the world, let alone our own bodies.

Perhaps the greatest tragedy of our education system is that we have instilled a sense of failure and a self-image as failure in extremely large numbers of children. In reality, these children are "canaries in the coal mine," indicators of a leaky poisonous gas that is affecting all of us. To violate the nature of children by forcing standards and behavior that are not suited to their developmental needs is cruel; to saddle them with blame and shame for the results is a tragedy.

Remember again to relax. Trust that your children are completely equipped to develop in astounding, wonderful ways. Give them the incredible gift of a relaxed, confident, unpressured environment in which to explore and grow. The result will be a young person who is relaxed, confident, and at ease, completely connected with you and with the world.

Remember the Importance of Rhythm

(A Second Alternative 3 Rs for Children: Rhythm, Routine, and Regularity)

My friend Donna Goertz, owner and director of Austin Montessori School, reviewed my booklet that was the precursor of the book you are reading now. She loved it and was most encouraging. At the same time, she pointed out one most significant area I had failed to address. Donna has worked with children for three decades and has raised two generations of her own biological children and step-children. Her observation has to do with RHYTHM.

Children need rhythm. They need routine. They need regularity. Donna bears witness to the unfortunate fact that large numbers of children today are sleep-deprived. Today's hectic world is one of working parents and attempts to meet adult individual needs within highly demanding schedules. In this world, what we see happening so often is that parents fail to establish a rhythm of regular routines for their children; dinners and bedtimes are all too often determined by parental needs and whims.

Although this makes our generation of parents sound irresponsible and selfish, I think much of this is actually a positive attempt to correct our own childhood experience of having been suppressed and controlled. For many of us, routine and regularity were there, but it was not a gentle, thoughtful and considerate establishment of rhythm in our lives. Many of us experienced a rigid and controlling imposition of our parents' will, coming from a place of anxiety, tension, anger and stress. The phenomenon of generational pendulum swings between authoritarian and permissive childrearing is common in families.

Consistency is important in establishing the rhythm necessary for your child to develop good, positive habits. At the same time, consistency is not a supreme value in and of itself. Someone once observed Mahatma Gandhi's inconsistencies and pointed them out to him in an accusatory tone. Gandhi's benign response was that the observer was accurate: that his commitment was to TRUTH, that truth was determined by the unique circumstances of each individual situation, and therefore was quite often not consistent.

Donna Goertz really brought home what I think is the key ingredient that must be added to bring forward the alchemical transformation that turns the base metal of consistency into a philosopher's stone of life-enhancing rhythm. Donna had just sent her youngest child to college; she was free to live a big part of her life according to her own desires. So what did she do? She fell in love with her current husband who happened to have two children of his own still many years away from leaving the nest. Donna made this choice from a place of experience (no naiveté here), and consciously embraced the need to continue determining a great part of her life according to the needs of the young people in her family. *Loving, conscious self-sacrifice, determined according to the needs of our developing children,* is the necessary approach to guide and complement consistency and create a healthy rhythm for your child. He will feel safe. She will thrive.

Remember that the intention of BioPsychiatry is to drug your child

The effect of this so-called treatment is to absolve the adults on whom your child depends of all responsibility. Once your child is labeled as defective and placed on drugs, then a STOP sign is placed on the need to figure out what might really be going on. The problem is defined as a sick child needing medicine—no need to look further.

Remember that these drugs are not a legitimate medical treatment of a medical disease or disorder from which your child suffers; that is a dangerous illusion. The drugs are a mechanism of social control and classroom engineering. All too often, their authentic function is to punish children who cannot or will not play the role we adults would like to impose on them.

Remember to NEVER GIVE UP

Labeling and drugging your child is a clear signal that adults have given up. Perhaps the most important thing you can ever do for a young person is to demonstrate again and again and again that you will never give up on him.

Remember to KEEP THINKING

Related to never giving up is to never stop thinking about the needs of your child; a parent's job never ends. Another of the most important things for young people to know is that you care enough to keep thinking as well of them as you possibly can. Mistakes are inevitable. *Children have no need for perfect parents; they need really good, imperfect parents who keep thinking and never give up.*

Remember to view your child through the EYES of DELIGHT

To see your child through the Eyes of Delight is the greatest gift in the world you can give to your child and to yourself. As with the feeling of urgency and pressure, viewing a child with anything other than delight really says more about the viewer than the child. Obviously children do experience distress and they do act this out; it means they need good attention from aware adults to help work something out. They are still inherently delightful. Adult responses of judgment and shame are not about the child; these responses are projections of feelings the adult carries inside himself.

Remember NOT to trust the thinking of anyone who sees your child through anything other than the eyes of delight. There really are no "bad" children. Your child is completely good and delightful.

PART II

Information and Action

CHAPTER 5
Four Crucial Ingredients

Resistance

"The secret of joy is resistance" [3]

Resist. Make it clear to school and mental health professionals that putting your child on psychiatric drugs is not an option. You are involved, you will participate, you will consider alternatives, but the use of toxic drugs that are dangerous to your child's brain, body, and soul is not open to discussion.

Support

Get SUPPORT for yourself. I'm not talking about support for your child, but *for you*. Parenting is an incredibly demanding job, and our society offers precious little by way of support. Figure out ways to get *practical* support such as child care, help with home responsibilities, transportation, etc. You also need *emotional* support. *Raising a child inevitably and without fail triggers your own distress*. It is the law that your own unresolved childhood issues will come up in dealing with your children.

This can place incredible stress on you. The best thing you can do for your child is to get help for yourself in the areas where it gets hard and you get emotionally activated. Explore and express thoughts and feelings coming

---

[3] This is the final line of Alice Walker's incredibly powerful novel on female circumcision, *Possessing the Secret of Joy*. Viewing this quotation, Leonard Frank suggested a wonderful corollary which is that "The secret of resistance is joy." I hope this book helps to reawaken the feeling of joy in your relationship with your child.

up for you in present time. If you think you need to seek professional help or attend a support or therapy group, do not hesitate to do so.

Get support specifically with the parenting experience. Parents listening to each other talk about parenting is incredibly valuable. Find other parents, and talk and listen. Sharing with other parents helps discover common ground and possible solutions, release feelings and receive validation and support. We tend to get extremely isolated as parents; it is so important and such a relief to connect with other parents. The best support and thinking I know of around children and parenting is through a grassroots peer counseling organization called Re-Evaluation Counseling (RC). This and other resources are listed at the end of this book.

Time

> "Nobody sees a flower—really—it is so small it takes time—we haven't time—and to see takes time, like to have a friend takes time." (Georgia O'Keeffe)

It has been said that *slowing down is the greatest act of civil disobedience one can commit in our society. Slow down and take time for your child.* Quality time is good, but much more important is just time. Young people need time to be nurtured, supported, loved and involved with you. They need enough time without pressure to show you their distress. If they can't get it out with you, where can they? For your sake and your child's, it is important that you create a relaxed atmosphere free of pressure.

All the forces of our market economy are geared to keep everyone going at an ever-increasing pace. It's profitable and counter-revolutionary. To quote my friend

Leonard Frank (personal communication), "Those who dare to slow down invite such labels as 'depression' (i.e., depressed or slowed activity). And off you go to the funny farm where the experts will try to get you up to speed again with—of all things—'speed,' which is not at all funny. . . . People who 'slow down' just may be reflecting. And to reflect seriously about one's place in society and about society itself is the beginning of wisdom."

For a child, slow time is essential. From a BioPsychiatric point of view and from a classroom teacher's point of view, daydreaming is as equally a "symptom" as is a high activity level. For a child, however, both are essential expressions of their naturally developing selves.

A Note on Punishment

I view punishment as mostly an act of despair. Isn't it tragic when relationships with our fellow human beings (and other life forms) degenerate into an interaction based on retribution and retaliation? Did you know that for a long time the United States has had by far the largest per capita prison population in all the world—easily exceeding the former USSR and South Africa in its heyday of Apartheid? Does this mean that we are the most primitive society in the world?

Isn't it especially tragic when we punish the ones we love the most and disregard our parental vows to honor, care for, love and nurture our children? Instead of a theological or metaphysical dogma on the nature of heaven and hell, I suggest we consider the following.

Heaven is seeing your child through the eyes of delight. A little bit of heaven is when you tenderly embrace and look adoringly into the eyes of your newborn baby.

Hell is when your vision is so distracted by demons that you see the sacred being who is your child as shameful and disgusting. You are in hell when you are overtaken by your own unhealed shame (the Devil) and fall victim to the tormenting emotions of embarrassment, anger and loathing. You are in hell when you buy into the lies that it is for your child's good that you be in this hell together and that you punish him for his wickedness.

I think the truth is that we punish our children when they need our love more than ever. When they are having a hard time and showing us their distress, they most certainly need our attention, but our loving and thoughtful attention.

Time is a huge factor in whether we punish our children. Responsible limit-setting and discipline require relaxed thought. Punishment, on the other hand, is easily done in haste and tension. Dan Jones' observation, and it tracks with my own, is that more than 90 percent of punishment incidents occur in situations where there is pressure about time. Check this out for yourself. Punishment tends to take place when a child is being forced to adhere to the adult's externally imposed schedule to be somewhere or get the child somewhere. I think we need to understand this and, given the pressures of modern-day life, view ourselves with compassion.

We know that prisons don't work except in a very narrow sense of removing someone from society; the prices we pay are enormous. One way to determine rationality is to look at whether there is flexibility to try other alternatives when something is not working. Our society's current response to disintegration is to keep building more prisons. Our society's response to failures in nurturing the development of our young people is to drug more of them.

I believe that punishment is not only tragic and pathetic, it simply doesn't work. Based on results, punishment begets more punishment, as well as fear, secrecy, shame and tense separation from the ones we are meant to love and cherish.

Down Time

It is important to allow our children down time. Constant activity and stimulation from radio, TV, video, computer, and other external sources allow no space for quiet and stillness needed for inner seedlings to grow.

Parents can help create this state by letting go of the belief that they are responsible for keeping their children busy and entertained. Consider the following dialogue:

Child: "I want to watch TV."
Parent: "No."
Child: "I'm bored. What are we going to do now?"
Parent: "Nothing."
Child: "I'm bored!" (restless, banging around, complaining. . .)
Parent: "I'm sure you'll think of something to do. . ., etc."

By placing the responsibility back on the child, one of two things will probably happen. Most of the time he will eventually pick something up or start drawing or reading or go outside and play. However, be prepared because sometimes it gets worse before it improves. If she is not used to down time, she will show withdrawal symptoms of irritability and crankiness. Try to wait it out, knowing that it will get better. By doing this, you are preparing fertile ground for your child's development. One other thing can happen that may look like withdrawal symptoms. Your child will use you as a counselor. I say more about this in the next section.

Special Time

All young people need special time alone with their parents, especially when they are having a hard time. This means that you, as a loving parent, care enough to set aside time (15 minutes, 30 minutes, 2 hours, 4 hours, every night, once a week or whatever you can do) from your busy life for you and your child to be alone together. During this time, *you do exactly what your child wants* (it's OK to set limits on spending money according to your resources), *and you are delightfully involved.* If anything gets in the way of your delightful involvement with your child, you will need to come back later and get support to work on the underlying cause.

Attention

Remember that "attention deficit disorder" is an extremely peculiar "disease" in which the distressing symptoms reside not in the "patient" but in the adults who interact with the "patient." It is useful to follow this awareness a bit further to propose the following maladies.

TADD—Teacher Attention Deficit Disorder[4]

Teaching is an incredibly difficult and undersupported job. A stressed teacher whose time and attention are overly taxed is more likely to have difficulty being flexible and creative enough to deal with demanding children.

As a parent, one thing you can do to support your children's teachers is to act as a counselor. Allow them to unload their complaints and difficulties on you; sympathize and give them all the encouragement and support you can.

---

[4] Thanks to Peter and Ginger Breggin for the TADD and DADD acronyms.

Keep in mind that a teacher who accepts the erroneous BioPsychiatric interpretation of children's behavior can be dangerous. Be firm and stand strong in your own decisions regarding your child's long-term welfare.

DADD - Dad Attention Deficit Disorder

Our society makes it extremely difficult for men to make time for their children, and fathers are often absent. I can only emphasize what an incredible difference it makes to a youngster to have his or her father actively interested and involved in his child's life. As a father, do everything you can to make this happen.

SADD - School/Societal Attention Deficit Disorder

Matthew Fox, Dominican priest, and major literary proponent of Creation Spirituality, said that "We are a nation that hates its enemies more than we love our young people." It is extremely sad, indeed, to give up on our children and drug them by the hundreds of thousands. No easy solutions here. As the Breggins pointed out in *War Against Children,* in raising children, there are many times for responsible adults when a decision must be made: EITHER SUPPRESS THE CHILD OR TRANSFORM THE WAY YOU DO YOUR LIFE.

On the Nature of Attention

I have deliberately played with the above acronyms in an attempt to shake loose the absurd belief that attention is a disordered deficit of a defective child. The fact that attention has become a commodity in our society, something we pay mental health professionals for, is a symptom not of mental illness, but of a distressed alienated society. Our lack of good available attention for our children is sad; let's tackle that problem, rather than label, stigmatize and drug our children.

I recently received a great gift that I want to share with you. It is a long excerpt from Julia Cameron's *The Artist's Way,* a profound statement about attention.

Very often, a creative block manifests itself as an addiction to fantasy. Rather than working or living the now, we spin our wheels and indulge in daydreams of could have, would have, should have. One of the great misconceptions about the artistic life is that it entails great swathes of aimlessness. The truth is that a creative life involves great swathes of attention. *Attention is a way to connect and survive.*

"Flora and fauna reports," I used to call the long, winding letters from my grandmother. "The forsythia is starting and this morning I saw my first robin. . . . The roses are holding even in this heat. . . . The sumac has turned and that little maple down by the mailbox. . . . My Christmas cactus is getting ready. . . ."

I followed my grandmother's life like a long home movie: a shot of this and a shot of that, sliced together with no pattern that I could ever see. "Dad's cough is getting worse. . . . The little Shetland looks like she'll drop her foal early. . . Joanne is back in the hospital at Anna. . . . We named the new boxer Trixie and she likes to sleep in my cactus bed—can you imagine?"

I could imagine. Her letters made that easy. Life through grandma's eyes was a series of small miracles: the wild tiger lilies under the cottonwoods in June; the quick lizard scooting under the gray river rock she admired for its satiny finish. Her letters clocked the seasons of the year and her life. She lived until she was eighty, and the letters came until the very end. When she died, it was as suddenly as her Christmas cactus: here today, gone tomorrow. She left behind her letters and her husband of sixty-two years. Her husband, my grandfather Daddy Howard, an elegant rascal with a gambler's smile and a loser's luck, had made and lost several fortunes, the last of them permanently. He drank them away, gambled them away, tossed them away the way she threw crumbs to her birds. He squandered life's big chances the way she savored the small ones. "That man," my mother would say.

My grandmother lived with that man in tiled Spanish houses, in trailers, in a tiny cabin halfway up a mountain, in a railroad flat, and, finally, in a house made out of ticky-tacky where they all looked just the same. "I don't know how she stands it," my mother would say, furious with my grandfather for some new misadventure. She meant she didn't know why.

The truth is, we all knew how she stood it. She stood it by standing knee-deep in the flow of life and paying close attention.

My grandmother was gone before I learned the lesson her letters were teaching: *survival lies in sanity, and sanity lies in paying attention.* Yes, her letters said, Dad's cough is getting worse, we have lost the house, there is no money and no work, but the tiger lilies are blooming, the lizard has found that spot of sun, the roses are holding despite the heat.

My grandmother knew what a painful life had taught her: success or failure, the truth of a life really has little to do with its quality. *The quality of life is in proportion, always, to the capacity for delight. The capacity for delight is the gift of paying attention.*

In a year when a long and rewarding love affair was lurching gracelessly away from the center of her life, the writer May Sarton kept *A Journal of a Solitude.* In it, she records coming home from a particularly painful weekend with her lover. Entering her empty house, "I was stopped by the threshold of my study by a ray on a Korean chrysanthemum, lighting it up like a spotlight, deep red petals and Chinese yellow center. . . . Seeing it was like getting a transfusion of autumn light."

It's no accident that May Sarton uses the word transfusion. The loss of her lover was a wound, and in her responses to that chrysanthemum, in the act of paying attention, Sarton's healing began.

The reward for attention is always healing. It may begin as the healing of a particular pain—the lost lover, the sickly child, the shattered dream. But what is healed, finally, is the pain that underlies all pain: the pain that we are all, as Rilke phrases it, "unutterably alone." *More than anything else, attention is an act of connection.*

Writing about attention, I see that I have written a good deal about pain. This is no coincidence. It may be different for others, but *pain is what it took to teach me to pay attention.* In times of pain, when the future is too terrifying to contemplate and the past too painful to remember, I have learned to pay attention to right now. The precise moment I was in was always the only safe place for me. Each moment, taken alone, was always bearable. *In the exact now, we are all, always, all right.* Yesterday the marriage may have ended. Tomorrow the cat may die. The phone call from the lover, for all my waiting, may not ever come, but just at the moment, just now, that's all right. I am breathing in and out. Realizing this, I began to notice that each moment was not without its beauty. (pp. 52-55, italics mine)

All this psychiatric hoopla about attention disorders is a great distortion and perversion of a very basic and fundamental human experience, an experience that Julia Cameron writes about in a particularly eloquent way. Our children are showing us their *pain*. As parents we are feeling *pain* related to our own struggles to live well in an extremely stressful society, and related to the anguish we feel when we see our children suffer.

Our children are hurting and we are hurting. On top of this, we feel fear in the midst of a highly fearful society; out of such fear comes the suppressive and despairing BioPsychiatric practice of putting our children on drugs. It truly is a tragic irony and perversion of the truth about attention to label children as attention-disordered and give them drugs. The irony is that we label pain as a disorder of the very quality we most need to heal—the quality of attention. Also an irony is that, as Cameron stated, *"pain is what it took to teach me to pay attention."* Our pain commands our attention. Our children's pain commands our attention. It seems to me that these "ADHD" children are forcing us to pay attention to them, to ourselves, and to the many ways in which our current ways of living and raising children cause pain. Let's not respond by suppressing the cries of our children. Let's do respond by paying attention; better yet, by *giving* our attention, freely and with love.

"Attention is a way to connect and survive." In essence, to pay attention to your child is to connect with and be in relationship with your child. Good, aware, loving attention is good, aware, loving relationship.

"The capacity for delight is the gift of paying attention." To see your child through the eyes of delight is the greatest gift you can give yourself and your child. It requires that you willingly pay the price of good attention. What you receive in return will be amazing. *"The reward for attention is always healing."*

CHAPTER 6
Five Very Special Gifts for Your Children

As stated, I strongly challenge the false assertions of BioPsychiatry which attempt to reduce the incredible nature of your children and the tremendous difficulties associated with school performance to biological and genetic abnormalities. I think it is a tragic mistake to act as if academic, behavioral and social challenges are a result of biological or genetic defects and to drug children with stimulants for "treatment" of those defects.

At the same time, it is important to know that behavior (including attention) cannot exist without its physiological, neurological and biochemical correlates, and that emotional distress greatly affects all these factors. I have already suggested ways to help children with emotional distress, and Part III is entirely devoted to this topic. Now I want to briefly mention four very specific, common-sense areas to examine in exploring ways to affect the biochemistry of your children in a positive way.

There is a simple law about being in a human body: *"What Goes In Must Come Out. The Quality of What Comes Out is Related to the Quality of What Goes In."* (Corollary: "Garbage in garbage out.")

This simple truth has profound implications. Once understood, it imparts great responsibility. I encourage you as parents to think of this responsibility as an opportunity to provide five very special gifts to yourselves and your children. These gifts are quality Food, Light, Sound, Talk and Touch.

Food

The place we have the greatest control and influence in the quality of our child's health, attention and behavior has to do with nutrition. The evidence is very clear that food affects health, mood and behavior. A lot has been written about the specific link between food and hyperactivity.

The amount of junk food that children in the United States eat is appalling. As a parent, you can help your child's biochemistry by restricting the following two items:

1) Sugar (in all its disguises)—white sugar, brown sugar, sucrose, fructose, corn syrup, etc. (Please note that substitutes such as Nutrasweet are also toxic and have been linked directly to problems with children.) (See Crook, 1991)

2) Chemical Additives and Preservatives—Read the labels and be selective.

You should be aware that some children have specific food allergies. These are often related to sugar and/or chemical additives, but can definitely include other foods. Dairy products, in particular, have been shown to be a major negative factor in many children's health and behavior. Always consider this where there are recurrent congestive problems or ear infections (Oski, 1977).

Encourage your children to eat fresh fruit. Fresh food is always the best choice. Select foods that are organic and free of pesticides and other chemicals and have received as little processing as possible. The closer the food to its whole, natural state, the more nutritious and healthy it is for your child. Whole grains and vegetables are good food for the body. I know from personal experience that it is extremely difficult to feed children well in a society that is so nutritionally out of balance. Do the best you can. It's worth the effort.

There are health providers who offer biochemical alternatives that may be helpful to your child. Doris Rapp, M.D. (1991) offers an allergy-extract therapy. Billie Jay Sahley, Ph.D. (1994) distributes a blend of vitamins, minerals, herbs and amino acids called "Calm Kids." Some parents swear by blue green algae. Homeopathic medicine has helped many children. Please see the references at the back of this book for information on resources.

My view is that it makes sense to think well about biochemistry. There is a dangerous tendency, however, to get just as caught up in the "alternative" biological treatments as we do with psychiatric biological treatments. A narrow focus on "fixing" a defective child, whether it be through psychopharmacology or through "natural" alternatives still tends to blame the child and move the helper away from acceptance and delight in the child, just as he is. It also distracts the helper from the big picture of other possibilities regarding life style, family, school and society. Please remember the essential nature of your child and his ongoing need and demand to fully express himself physically, emotionally and verbally.

It is important to know that suppression of emotion or behavior does alter biochemistry. Similarly, release of suppressed feeling or action often affects a profound healing alteration of deranged biochemistry.

Light

Along with the rising incidence of so-called "attention disorders," you may have noticed that more and more Americans are wearing glasses (I've heard estimates of 70 percent), and an increasing number of children are experiencing vision problems. Not long ago Americans spent 90 percent of their time outdoors. Today, the average U.S. citizen spends 97 percent of his time indoors.

Research indicates that the quality of light in a classroom directly affects attention and behavior (see Liberman, 1991). We certainly know it affects the eyes. It is recommended that we keep TV and video watching at a minimum and remember that a computer screen has a similar effect on the eyes. Make sure your children spend as much time outdoors as possible. Give them the gift of full-spectrum light!

Sound

How often has your child experienced the gift of quiet? Or sat in a place free of man-made noise and listened to the wind and the water and other sounds in nature? I realize many of us in the cities cannot easily provide this gift, but it is so important.

Research and experience have clearly demonstrated the effects of sound on mood, behavior, health, thinking and learning (see Halpern, 1985). Please do the best you can to provide your child as much time as possible in an environment where the quality of sound is calm, quiet, soothing, peaceful.

Our children are greatly over-stimulated. This over-stimulation interferes with their ability to be self-directed, with the quality of their awareness and attention, and with their physiology, neurology and biochemistry. An over-stimulated mind and body cannot rest, does not know calm. It's true that children love excitement; give them that. You can do your child a great service, however, by providing time in an environment with good food, good light and good sound. This is healthy stimulation.

Talk

As Jane Healy describes it in her book *Endangered Minds,* talk is "the magic formula." Conversation builds the "executive brain." In order to sustain attention and concentration, young people must have experienced the "rich broth of language and reflection." This "inner speech" experience, or mental dialogue with one's self, is necessary to develop a capacity for personal thought and problem solving.

It is really quite simple. You must *talk* with your child—a lot! Help your children talk and think their way through a problem. Adults must act as coaches to show children how to internalize speech, as this teaches them strategies for thinking. Personal thought and problem solving result.

There are at least three prerequisites for the development of inner speech and the executive brain. First is quiet. A child must have time in an environment free of over-stimulating background noise and programming. Second is competent and caring adults to act as coaches. You model reflective thought and coach your child, asking questions that will help her think through problems. Third, you listen.

By listening to and drawing out your child's own thinking, you provide support and encourage independence. This mutually shared responsibility creates a learning environment that is optimal for your child's development.

A recent interaction with my daughter, Vanessa, provides an example of what I mean by coaching your child on reflective thought. Vanessa found my hammer and started banging around the house. Fortunately I had some available attention, so rather than reacting by ordering an immediate return of my tool, I asked what she was doing. With a slight tone suggesting how stupid I was for asking such a question, she said "I'm hammering." A pleasant reply of "I'm working" would not have been unusual. Either way, if your attention is good, you're in good shape to keep asking questions. You may ask, "How's it going?" She may respond with "Good." or she may ignore you. You might ask, "What do you do with a hammer?" She might answer, "Hit with it." or "Hammer." or "Build something."

My interaction with Vanessa went something like this.

Vanessa: I want to build something.

Dad: Good idea! What do you need?

Vanessa: Nails.

Dad: We don't have any.

Vanessa: Oooh, pooh.

Dad: What can we do?

Vanessa: Go buy some?

Dad: Great idea. When we pick up your brother we'll go to the hardware store. (At the store, Vanessa picks out the nails she wants with discussion of size and amount. We return home and she goes out to build with her brother, Eric, who has an ongoing treehouse/fort project. Momentarily she returns.)

Vanessa: I can't find any wood.

Dad: For what?

Vanessa: I want to build a prayer.

Dad: What?

Vanessa: A prayer.

Dad: What do you mean?

Vanessa: (She shows me with her arms. Eric notices

	and knows immediately she means a cross.)
Dad:	Aha! Is there any wood for that?
Vanessa:	I can't find any.
Dad:	What about that old chair that's falling apart?
Vanessa:	(Vanessa checks and comes back with a report on why it's unsatisfactory.)
Dad:	How about asking your brother.
Vanessa:	(She goes out again and in a little while returns with a completed "prayer.")

I'll conclude this section by quoting Kenneth Klivington, editor of *The Brain, Cognition and Education*. When asked how he would advise parents, he immediately responded:

> I continue to place the emphasis on the *need to generate language and thought, not just listen and watch*. If we consider the brain as an organ of thought, it has to be structured to work right. If you don't wire your computer right, it isn't going to work right.

A Special Note On TV

By now you have no doubt realized that I see television as a harmful technology. The average American spends five hours daily in front of the TV, making TV watching, after work and sleep, the main activity everyday in many of our lives. For five hours every day, we choose to watch instead of participate. The average child spends 1,680 minutes per week watching TV. In contrast, the number of minutes per week that parents spend in meaningful conversation with their children is 38.5. The pervasive use of TV makes it probably the greatest single influence on our young people's lives today. What a shame.

I am not talking about the content. Much has been said about the violence, sex, advertising, insanity and values of TV programming—PBS or MTV, sports or drama, sex or sitcom, no matter. Nor am I talking about the insidious and conscienceless manipulation of young people's minds by a corporate world whose primary guiding value is and always will be a profit motive, although I do address it later. What I am talking about is the very act of watching *any* TV.

My purpose is to draw your attention to the fundamental nature of the technology and how it acts on the minds of children. I will use three of the subtitles from Jerry Mander's chapter on TV as audiovisual training in his book, *In the Absence of the Sacred*.

Freedom of Speech for the Wealthy

This point is quite simple. Only the largest corporations in the world dominate the broadcast signals for the obvious reason that only they can afford it. TV is a private system in the hands of the largest corporations. Freedom of speech in TV broadcasting could not be further from the truth; it is no more than an illusion for the general public. Mander shares the most shocking statistic:

> The average American who watches five hours of television per day sees approximately 21,000 commercials per year.

This translates into 21,000 identical messages about life, all aggressively saying, "Buy something—do it now!"

The Technology of Passivity

The fact that TV is on for an average of eight hours a day in American homes is proof of its hypnotic quality. The term "Zombie" has been used by many parents to describe TV's effects on their children. Scientists have studied this phenomena and found that the brain slips into an "alpha" brainwave mode after watching TV. This is a noncognitive mode, meaning no thinking, no filtering. Information can be placed *directly* into the mind, *without* viewer participation.

Mander cites three reasons why TV viewing causes the brain to slip into this mode. One is the lack of eye movement. When an image does not have to be sought, a key aspect of mental stimulation is lost. The second factor, according to psychologists who use hypnotism, is that TV very effectively induces a hypnotic trance. Looking at a flickery TV screen (60x/second) is just like staring at a hypnotist's candle.

Mander considers his third factor most important. Images come from the TV screen at their own speed as an image "stream" outside the viewer's control. No pulling out images. No contemplation. No active participation. If you attempt to do so, you fall behind.

In order to watch TV, you have to surrender to the images; you must allow the images to enter at their speed. The only other choice is to withdraw from the experience.

Comparing television viewing to the use of drugs, Mander concludes that TV has many of the characteristics of Valium and other tranquilizers. He goes on to say that this is only half the story, however. If TV is a drug, says Mander, it is not really Valium, it is *Speed*. For our purposes, the equation goes like this:

TV is Speed
Ritalin is Speed
Therefore, TV is Ritalin

Acceleration of the Nervous System

I conclude this section on the effects of TV viewing by quoting Mander on how TV directly promotes hyperactivity.

> In their famous study of the effects of television, researchers at Australian National University predicted that as television became more popular in Australia, there would be a corresponding increase in hyperactivity among children. I found this prediction alarming because many parents of hyperactive children place their kids in front of the television set, where they seem to calm down. Apparently, the opposite effect is what finally results.
>
> Here's how it works: While sitting quietly in front of the TV, the child sees people punching each other on the screen. There is the impulse to react as the fight-or-flight instinct is activated, but since it would be absurd to react to a television fight, the child suppresses the emotion. As the fighting continues, so does the cycle of impulse and suppression. Throughout the television-viewing experience, the child is drawn back and forth on this see-saw of action and suppression, all the while appearing zapped and inactive. When the set goes off, this stored-up energy bursts forth in the disorganized, frantic behavior that we associate with hyperactivity. Often, the only calming act is to again put the set on, which starts the cycle anew.

Please consider that TV trains children for drug and commodity dependencies. I very highly recommend that you read Mander's work (see references) and allow yourself to think the unthinkable: *What about the elimination of television?*

I saw a client recently whose presenting problem was a scuffle with her husband over a gun when she threatened to shoot their TV. When presented with a similar dilemma, Swami Beyondananda (Steve Bhaerman, *New Texas Magazine*) recommended that the couple go ahead and shoot the TV. His advice was to substitute two hours of television each evening with two hours of Tell-A-Vision in which family members take turns sharing their dreams and visions for life. What a gift!

Jane Healy, in her book *Endangered Minds,* concludes a chapter called "Sesame Street and the Death of Reading" this way:

> Children immersed from birth in the spicy sensory bouillabaisse of visual immediacy will not become readers unless they have also soaked up the Rich Broth of Language and Reflection. Preschoolers who have been sold gimmicks in the name of learning and school-age children whose needs are habituated to the easy pleasures of viewing may well find the culture of school an alien one. Their brains, shaped by visual novelty, may gradually lose the ability to bend themselves intelligently around the written word. (P. 234)

Leonard Frank has written a lot on thinking and propaganda and brainwashing. His most recent publication is called *Influencing Minds: A Reader in Quotations.* After reading the above section on TV, Leonard wrote: "TV promotes hyperactivity. No doubt about it. It's also a marvelous brainwashing tool. It gives you no time to think, unlike books which because they allow you to use them at your own pace are a great aid to reflection, knowledge, self-knowledge and wisdom. Descartes once wrote *(Discourse on Method,* 1637) 'The reading of good books is like conversing with the best people of earlier times!' What better way to sharpen our wits and raise our consciousness."

Touch

Jean Liedloff, in *The Continuum Concept,* coined a phrase that puts a name on something that deeply affects most of us as parents. It's called "In-Arms Deprivation." What this means is that we are deeply affected by our unmet need to be held as babies. Babies need to be held constantly in the first six months of life, and a great deal of the time thereafter. Fortunately we have recovered some from the professional advice that our own parents received, which was to leave babies in their cribs, let them cry themselves to sleep, feed them on schedule, etc. However, this fact of our own upbringing, together with the busyness and demands of life, still makes it very difficult for us to wholeheartedly meet the needs of our children. The way to spoil children is by neglecting their needs. *Always remember that meeting a child's needs is all to the good.*

Another "alternative" treatment of "ADHD" is a type of physical therapy called Sensory Integration (Ayres, 1979) which involves a lot of movement and physical contact. My own limited anecdotal evidence suggests it can be helpful. My problem with this and other approaches such as "neurotherapy" (EEG brain wave biofeedback) is that they tend to be based on the premise that not only is there a legitimate difference between children, but that the ones called "ADHD" are "pathological" and need to be corrected back to "normal." Thus, the physical therapy is not framed as a way of responding to a basic human need for touch and contact, or to deficits or hurts around touch and closeness. Rather, the problem is "tactile defensiveness" which sounds very clinical pathological to me. The actual modalities of movement—touching, banging, crashing, jumping, chewing, etc.,—are great. My main warning is once again about labeling your child's unique expressions as a clinical disorder; the subsequent tendency is to relate to her as an object or a syndrome, rather than as a unique, delightful young person.

It should also be noted that many young people, just as adults, derive great benefit from massage. Craniosacral work which involves manipulation guided by the craniosacral pulse or rhythm has been reported to help many children. Of particular interest with this work is that it often addresses and helps with problems specifically related to the effects of trauma suffered as a result of compression during birth. So do what will help and be aware. My advice is that you touch, hold, embrace, squeeze, cuddle, snuggle, wrestle with your child. Keep reaching for closeness. This is especially crucial for boys. Male oppression sets in very early and causes boys to push you away and isolate in their distress. Let them push and show their hurts, but *don't ever believe that they really don't want to be close. They do, desperately!* Keep reaching in. Tell them it's your need, but you just can't help it!

We must not abandon our children to the distressful patterns of isolation that they will show us. Remember to see your child through the Eyes of Delight. Know that deep inside they really do want to be completely close to you. Have fun with it. Keep reaching in for your sweet child.

PART III

*On Counseling
Children*

CHAPTER 7
Brief Theory And Tips

This part of the book, On Counseling Children, is the heart of what I offer to you. This chapter contains theory and tips from the teachings of Re-Evaluation Counseling, a grassroots peer counseling organization which has developed some of the clearest thinking I have seen anywhere on children and parenting.

Theory

1) Human beings are inherently zestful, intelligent, loving, and cooperative.

2) When human beings are hurt physically or emotionally, they experience distress. This distress is then recorded and stored in the body, and interferes with all the above qualities of our inherent nature (that is, we become less intelligent and cooperative).

3) Fortunately, human beings have a built-in mechanism for healing from the effects of having been hurt. This mechanism can be called emotional discharge; our hurt is healed by expressing our feelings.

4) Children will use their parents as a primary resource to express themselves if it feels safe and their parents support them.

Tips

1) Know that children (like adults) are not "reasonable" when upset. They generally don't "talk it out."

2) Your attention is essential. Counsel your child when you feel pretty awake and aware. Don't try to counsel your child when you are emotionally upset, over-tired or distracted by other concerns.

3) Emotional expression (crying, shaking from fear, angry talk) is not the hurt, it is the release of the hurt. We often confuse the hurt with the release of the hurt. When a child cries, for example, (unless she is in acute response to pain such as being stuck by a diaper pin), she is releasing a hurt that was already there before she cried. The emotional discharge, the expression of the feelings, is what allows the child to heal from the hurt.

4) Do not interfere with the discharge by trying to get the child to laugh or be distracted, by shaming the child for showing feelings, or in any other way. Instead, relax, stay close, encourage discharge. Keep reaching in. Know that your child wants to be completely close to you. It is only the distress that makes the child push you away (or makes you want to get away!).

5) Remember that when a child shows anger that he really doesn't want to hurt anyone or anything. Protect your child from doing harm and be confident that she is doing what she can to express some really difficult feelings.

6) Few in our parents' generation had this information, so few of us were supported to express ourselves emotionally. Doing this for your child will not be easy. *Counsel your child, but get help when you feel that the job is more than you can handle by yourself.*

A Note on Seeking Professional Help

If you decide to get professional help, be sure you know the approach and perspective of those you consider. Ask the professionals tough questions about how they see children and families. Make sure they wholeheartedly support your decision to avoid drugging your child. Make sure that they think about young people in a way that really makes sense and is consistent with what you are doing as a parent. Expect complete respect for you and your child.

CHAPTER 8
Shame: A Legacy of Misery

Shame is the awful feeling that you are bad, wicked, defective, incompetent, or in some way fundamentally flawed. Shame is the belief not that you did something wrong, but that there is something wrong with you. Shame is the worst feeling in the world. It feels so bad you just want to hide. John Bradshaw (1988), in his book *Healing the Shame That Binds You,* clued me into this. A defining characteristic of shame is that it feels unbearable to be exposed. Shame thrives as a hidden secret and compels the bearer to isolate and avoid confrontive situations that threaten to expose the unbearable feeling and conviction of fundamental worthlessness. So how does a child acquire this terrible feeling that he is flawed and defective? How does a child come to carry a conviction that she is bad, wrong and undeserving? It comes from outside.

Instilling Shame: On the Psychodynamics of Abuse

Alice Miller (1990) presents one of the clearest explanations of the psychodynamics of child abuse. According to Miller, children see themselves as the responsible centers of the universe and their parents as omnipotent and all-knowing. Lacking the information and power available to adults, when a child is hurt by a parent, the child unavoidably internalizes the experience. Strangely enough, the child internalizes *both* sides of the experience, as victim and as powerful adult perpetrator. Naturally, the primary identification is that of victim, afraid and ashamed. When a child is not supported and not allowed to express and work through the effects of such a hurt, he will protect himself intrapsychically through the mechanism of "splitting." This means that in order to function without feeling constantly overwhelmed by fear and shame, the child will "split off" the internalized experience of being a powerless, terrified victim and banish this knowledge as deeply as possible into the unconscious mind. Just as it is natural for a child to initially see herself as a terrified victim, it is equally natural that, given a later opportunity, that same child will choose to identify with a powerful perpetrator in a relational world in which abusive inequities of power are the norm. The final psychodynamic of this process is that the split-off internalized victim self is projected from the unconscious depths of the psyche onto the other person in an interaction. We feel bad deep inside, but long ago learned how to protect ourselves by keeping the feelings deep down out of conscious awareness. *So instead of recognizing and owning our shame, we turn around and blame another, one who is weaker, less powerful. We project our shame onto our child.*

The process includes four stages: (1) An act of abuse, (2) internalization of both sides of that abusive interaction, (3) splitting and unconscious denial of victimization, and (4) projection of the denied powerless and shame-filled victim self. Now the stage is set for re-enactment and perpetuation of the abusive pattern. To the individual who unconsciously projects his own internalized terror and shame onto another, that other is bad and powerless, fully deserving and in need of correction. The original victim acts on such a conviction and is fully justified in whatever act is perpetrated. The cycle of abuse is complete.

My description of Alice Miller's psychodynamic inter-pretation of abuse emphasizes shame as a potent factor in human relations. The child always carries a heavy load of shame. Viewing the world from a responsible center, a child naturally accepts and believes a parent's assertion by word and action that the child is deserving of whatever abuse the parent commits. He naturally accepts whatever labels and "treatments" the adults of the systems in which he is involved give him.

That we are able to transform the moral language of "bad, wicked, sinful child" to that of "needy, dependent, biogenetically defective ADHD mental patient" conceals the above dynamic. The core emotional states of fear and shame are unaltered in this translation and reside in the experience of powerlessness and helplessness. Fear and shame remain fully intact in the "patient" child/profes-sional interactional dynamics of our coercive education and mental health systems.

A distorted view of human nature makes it easier to perpetuate the legacy of shame by providing wonderful protection against the inevitable tinges of discomfort that surface in the midst of harmful activity. Adultism is per-fectly fine when children are seen as born in original sin, or fundamentally lazy and unmotivated, or as untamed animals needing to be civilized. Our education and men-tal health systems can easily perpetuate shame and do great harm without having to agonize in guilt, without feeling their own shame. They can put two million of our children on Ritalin without qualm; all that is necessary is to be convinced that these massive numbers of young people are inherently flawed, biologically and genetically defective.

Theodore Roszak (1992), in his book on EcoPsychology, argues that this quality of shame, manifested as a guilty conscience and fundamental distrust of self, is absolutely necessary to ensure that humans operate as cogs in a system that is basically anti-human. According to Roszak,

> The politics of domination begins when some people teach other people that the body, the psyche, the community, and nature-at-large are unreliable, incompetent, hostile, therefore in need of top-down supervision. *Authoritarian politics roots itself as the guilty conscience.* It begins by convincing people they cannot trust one another, that they cannot trust themselves. (p. 230) (italics mine)

Our competitive system of compulsory age-segregated education is designed to fulfill this function well. What Roszak is really talking about here is now commonly referred to as a feeling of shame. He quotes Gary Snyder, ecology's poet laureate, to summarize the issue:

> A ruling class, to survive, must propose a Law: a law to work must have a hook into the social psyche—and *the most effective way to achieve this is to make people doubt their natural worth and their instincts, especially sexual.* To make 'human nature' suspect is also to make Nature—the wilderness—the adversary. Hence the ecological crisis of today. (p. 230)

And hence the crisis and "War Against Children" today. Our Judeo-Christian heritage does much of the work. Shame-based child rearing creates the interpersonal dynamics. Our mental health system with its BioPsychiatric basis fits right in. And shame is a steel thread that powerfully reinforces it all.

On Shame and Suppressing Our Children's Joy and Zest

It is humbling and saddening to realize that an inevitable result of our carrying shame is that we suppress our children. Just as it feels unbearable to expose shame, it also feels unbearable to be around shameless people. *When we are carrying shame, it is unbearable to be around people who are zestful and enthusiastic and love life and unconditionally love themselves. Exuberant joy in our children is excruciating!*

Why is this? Remember that shame is the most awful feeling in the world. Remember that we split it off, banish it into our unconscious to protect ourselves. Remember that shame thrives in secrecy, that it feels unbearable to be exposed. Remember that we were shamed not only for our defiant self-defense, but for our exuberance and enthusiasm. Take a look at how your own family of origin handled "bragging," how you feel about singing your own praises. Shame is attached to all the feelings we need to express in order to heal. The many prohibitions, punishments and admonitions against expressing our feelings when we were children make it very difficult for us to do so now. Each time we release our buried feelings, we also experience the ugly shame that is bound to these feelings, making recovery work all the more difficult.

It was not only the so-called negative feelings that were bound in shame. So was the joy, the zest, the exuberance, the enthusiasm! We were shamed for *all* our feelings. The result is that we can hardly stand it now when our naturally outrageous, dynamic and enthusiastic children hold themselves out as the most valuable center of the universe.

The Way Out: Complete Self-Appreciation

It makes sense, then, that it's hard to see our children through "The Eyes of Delight" when they're showing us their distress or their zest. What I want you to consider now is that it is vital to delight in their delight!

The way out is simple. Yet it is probably the most profound, powerful, difficult and challenging tool we have in our recovery. It is to ruthlessly expose the shame, to give no quarter to embarrassment. And the most effective way to accomplish this is, as Walt Whitman modeled, to sing "A Song of Myself." To proudly and joyfully sing our own praises is to challenge every bit of shameful conditioning we've received from our families, our churches, our schools, all of our socio-cultural heritage. *The fact is that we must delight in and love ourselves unconditionally in order to truly delight in and appreciate our children. The alternative is to suppress them so that we won't feel so bad.*

Dan Jones, counselor and writer, has been my best teacher and model for becoming "Shameless." I want to share with you now a poem he wrote last year that carries that title.

Shameless
by Dan Jones

Elders are shocked.
Preachers fall out of their pulpits.
Mothers stop their children's ears.
But it's true and I'll say it:

I am head-over-heels in love with myself,
starry-eyed crazy about Me, my own Self.
Pouring rapturous praises over myself,

I crown myself with laurels,
pin on rows of medals,
grin and strut and crow
until Shame itself is scandalized.

Vanity and conceit have nothing to do with this,
and not arrogance or righteousness.
Those are the masks of Shame.
The "proud" man, the "vain" woman,
the smug, the selfish, the egotistical and stuck-up,
all the "better-than,"
the know-it-alls and judges and busybodies,
inside they squirm with unworthiness worms
and have no love for themselves.

Self-love is good-humored and easygoing.
A self-loved body tingles with pleasure
like a sun-warmed beach
when waves of love wash over.
A self-loved mind is at peace,
does not turn against itself in criticism,
does not strive to make up for itself with a good show,
is content with itself, and therefore
has no fear, no anger, no greed,
no hurry, no worry,
just glides along like a white cloud
doing one thing at a time
as though it were serious.

Self-love is the spring, the source of all the rivers of love that
    flow.
It is the hive for all the honey,
the store for all the presents.
It is a home of God.

It is not "attention-getting."
It is not at anyone's expense.
It is free for all.
It is everyone's birthright.

Unconditional,
it cannot be earned or achieved.
It's not because of anything,
it's just there, like space,
and it moves throughout the body
like a river of light.

Self-love is not different from humility.
Humility means going easy on myself
about achievements and image,
the puffed-up masks and costumes,
the dramas to stage myself
and be seen as the star of the show.
Humility means giving myself a rest
from the rush against time,
the endless, busy river
of explanations and justifications
and compensations and rationalizations
and stupefying lists of projects
for self-improvement and doing good,
none of them ever enough,
never enough, never enough,
hurry along, there's more to do,
more to do, more to do.
Self-love has enough already,
delights to give itself away
like an ice cream machine overflowing.
Self-love "versus" love-of-others
is a treachery to the heart.
Love radiates.
Without self-love,
what is there to radiate?

How many grim relationships we endure
to try to get the love we fail to give ourselves,
sucking at a dry breast
when the milk is flowing in our own hearts.
Why should we have to wait for a lover to fall in love?

So here it is! Your full pardon from the Governor. It reads:
'My life might need some work,
but I myself, the worker on my life,
am forever immaculately perfect.'
Frame it. Hang it in your mind.
Never surrender your Freedom
from the dismal prison of Shame.

• • • •

Now the economists are alarmed.
If this should spread, they wonder,
who would buy what and why?
Whole industries gasp
at the specter of a less needy nation.
The cosmetic and fashion industries faint.

Mad. Avenue unleashes
barrages of TV commercials
with beautiful unloved models
fretting about odors and hairs
and other people's possible opinions,
to keep us all shamed and needy and buying
buying shiny new machines
and sex and beer and remission of sins.

But people turn off the TVs,
grow gardens and sing love songs,
admire simplicity and cultivate love.

Holy hookahs! The money we'll save on drugs
when we sip at the spring of natural ecstasy.
The Drug Enforcement Agency
will look like the Maytag repairman.
Pastors brighten their sermons
since no one will ever submit
to another harangue.
Lawyers, to keep busy,
are reduced to suing each other.
Republicans quote Thomas Jefferson.
Nazis and Klansmen march against each other.

Divorce courts are made into museums
as people no longer marry to 'find' love
but to celebrate it in each other.

And this is the way the world will heal:
not by making people 'good'
but by letting us fall in love.

• • • •

Old renegade that I am,
I will not stop at blasphemy.
I commit sacrilege
before the high altar of Shame
and proclaim the shocking sin
of my own magnificent wonderfulness.
If I ever die, it will be from
loving myself to death.

I would like a lot more company here.
Come, let us luxuriate,
let us slow down and rejoice in ourselves,
let us bathe ourselves in praise,
lavishly, extravagantly,
adoring and shameless,
until Shame itself suffers a fatal embarrassment,
blushes such a furious fiery-red blush,
it's consumed in its own flame and self-cremates.
We keep the ashes for a souvenir
Final score: Self-love: 100
                 Shame: 0

And this is a victory poem,
celebration and call.
We've passed the final exam,
school is out and it's all vacation.
Strike up the band! Throw away the drugs.
Our team won and it's Love for us forever!
Parade up and down every street and hall.
We have it all! We have it all!

102

CHAPTER 9
Basic Principles and Phenomena

Three of the most important and challenging areas in which young people need our counseling help are (1) Crying, (2) Working on Fear, and (3) Anger. Before discussing these, however, I want to stress some basic principles that parents and other adults working with young people need to understand.

First and foremost, always remember that this job of caring for and supporting the development of our young people is profoundly significant, important and valuable. This *may* seem obvious and in truth it is obvious; yet it seems that much of the function (based on results) of modern urban-industrial existence is to obscure the obvious. One of the best ways to create obscurity and confusion is to say one thing and do another—the old "Do as I say, not as I do." Double messages to children create great distress, uncertainty and confusion: a parent who says "I love you" while a tone of voice and posture reveals an inner experience of tense anger; a teacher who lectures again and again on respect, but is condescending and patronizing in tone and action. Another pointed example is a society that extols "family values" while at the same time failing to provide for the needs of families and young people. There is *very* little slack, very little flexibility, very little financial support for us *as parents*. Based on a look at resource allocation, Matthew Fox, American theologian and writer, has said that "We are a nation that hates our enemies more than we love our young people." Similarly, I would say that we are a nation not of family values, but of corporate values; rather than well-supported parents and sweetly cared for young people, the bottom line is corporate profit.

The point of all this is to acknowledge two related truths:

(1) Parenting is a crucially important and valuable job, and

(2) There is precious little support in our society for the job of parenting.

This second truth is especially important to remember when it gets really hard and we fail to act according to the standards we hold for ourselves as parents. When we're frustrated, impatient, scolding, disrespectful, patronizing, sarcastic, lacking good attention, we tend to forget what a good job we've done, what sacrifices we're making, how tired we are, what we're up against. We are apt to judge ourselves and conclude that it's hard because something is wrong with us. The truth is that much of the time it's hard not because something is wrong with us, but because it's just plain hard. And it's especially hard because we are parenting in the context of a society that is highly distressed and generally not conducive to quality parenting and meeting family needs. You're doing a good job; no doubt you are passing on to your children as few of your own hurts as you possibly can.

A Death Walk for Parents

Another basic phenomenon is that much of what we see in this world is backward or upside down, like a mirror that reflects reality in a distorted way. Remember that we are still coming out of a legacy that views the natural world and the nature of human beings as flawed and sinful. The recent history of advice on how to care for children is founded on the belief that human nature is basically bad: lazy, undisciplined, wild, irresponsible, selfish, etc. Children must be tamed and civilized. Deep distrust and fear drive our desperate need to *control* our young people.

While small segments of our society have made great progress in contradicting this conventional wisdom and our unconscious conditioning, there is still great pressure to "control your child." Looks and gestures of disapproval from others are not uncommon when you allow your child to complain, to tantrum, to whine, to talk back to you. Control or suppression of emotional expression is still a primary value in our society. What I propose in counseling our young people violates this value. To allow, honor, and encourage emotional expression in our young people is a direct affront to external and internal advocates of emotional denial and self-control. The teaching that emotional expression is a natural, built-in mechanism for healing the effects of being physically or emotionally hurt is not well understood or accepted by most of our society.

Be prepared for a challenge. It takes great strength to violate a group norm or expectation. As an illustration, Arnold Mindell (1993) tells the story of a powerful, tribal mountain group that forced any member who violated a group law or norm to undergo a "Death Walk." The offender had to pass through a gauntlet of tribal members who took shots at him. One unlikely way to survive the Death Walk was if all the gunshot wounds did not kill you. Of particular interest was the rare individual who could "walk in such a way that the group members could not pull the trigger." How to walk in such a way is not clear. I suggest that, as a parent, it means clearing enough of your own shame that others' criticism of your parenting does not "kill" you.

Be prepared to receive some shots—of judgment, disapproval, doubt, and skepticism from others in your social group. Expect your own internal critics to begin shooting away at you as well with self-criticism, self-doubt, and that most distressing feeling of all, unhealed shame.

The Principle of Unraveling Suppression

Be warned that, once you decide to challenge the norm, *it may very well get a lot worse before it gets much better.* I haven't yet come up with the best name for this phenomenon, so I have called it "The Principle of Unraveling Suppression." When matter or energy is compressed, a powerful, potential force is created that needs to be released to avoid an explosion, the way a pressure cooker allows steam to escape. In order to heal, we must release or discharge our hurtful experiences through emotional expression. Hurt and loss are healed by crying; fear by shaking, trembling and sweating; anger by heat and vociferous expression; physical pain and tension by yawning. When a child's natural inclination to express feelings in these ways is suppressed, order and surface calm may eventually appear; *the hurt, however, does not go away, even after many years.*

A part of the child may go into a chronic shock condition involving constricted awareness, emotional numbing and restricted range of emotional expression. Chronic physical tension and/or chronic alteration of physiological arousal systems will often occur. Limitations on the child's naturally flexible and creative intelligence are part and parcel of unhealed hurts. Suppression of feelings takes its toll.

When the door is opened, when the pressure valve is released, it can get quite messy. Reactions appear to be over-reactions, out of proportion to present time events, as they often are. A child is denied an ice cream cone and acts as if it were the end of the world. As a parent, you are accused by your child of all manner of evil intent and told that you don't care, that you *never* give her anything, that it's *all* your fault, that she *hates* you, and so forth.

But if you understand that your child is using you as a counselor to work on unresolved feelings of denial, frustration or rejection, then you can help your child enormously. When you are able to remain calm and loving, your child will heal through her stormy behavior. Remember that, no matter what she is saying, deep down she dearly loves you; she's simply working out some distress.

Your Child Will Use You

Human beings are extremely intelligent; young people are brilliant. They know, at a very deep level, to take advantage of good adult attention when it is available. Offer this to your child, and your child's natural intelligence and built-in mechanisms for healing will combine to take full advantage of this gift. He will use the slightest pretext (e.g., you cut his pancake the "wrong" way) to express pain around a whole legacy of hurts and disappointments. Some of these may be past experiences with you; many you actually had nothing to do with. You may or may not discover the sources. Most likely you won't, but it really doesn't matter. What does matter is that you are assisting your child to release and heal the many hurts associated with the slings and arrows of outrageous fortune, the insults, frustrations and disappointments of a small being in an adult-oriented world. All this will test your mettle; I guarantee it. You will react and be imperfect, but don't be hard on yourself. Remember that you are doing important work, handling a very tough job in a very tough situation. Commend yourself for all you are doing.

Safety

One final piece remains to be considered in regard to this phenomenon of your children "taking out" their problems on you. As I've already mentioned, a child, (and an adult for that matter) will use the safest person in her life to show and work on her greatest distresses, the places where it's really hard. Children (and adults) need safety in order to heal and grow. When it comes to letting it all hang out, it's going to be with Mom or Dad. Think about it this way: *if not you, then who?* Again, the outside is upside down from the inside. Oftentimes, what looks and feels like disrespect is really a gift of trust coming from a place of safety built on the child's knowing that you have shown him respect. He is using you as a counselor because you are the safest person in his life. I know this is difficult and an ongoing challenge. It's good to model respect. It's also good to expect respect. Consider, however, that when a child is using you as a counselor, that is not the time to think about courtesy and manners. Interrupting disrespectful patterns is good; they don't serve your child. Nevertheless, resist the urge to dismiss or suppress your child's need to work this stuff out with you. I'll say more about this in the upcoming section on anger. For now, consider giving yourself permission to be a little loose around the edges with all this. I know how hard it is. Good Luck!

CHAPTER 10
Crying

I have already said that tears are the release of hurt. Well, what about the complaining, the whining, the moaning, the groaning, the howls, the screeches, the sobs and all the rest? Although we've made some progress in the last two generations in allowing children to express their feelings, we still have a long way to go. Such expressions as "Big boys don't cry," "Stop that whining," "Crybaby," "Be a big girl," "Stop crying or I'll give you a reason to cry about," and "Go to your room and come out when you're decent to be around," are still commonplace in our society.

That's what's on the outside. What's inside is especially challenging, often excruciating, for most of us. Think about yourself. How do you feel when a baby is crying or screaming? Is it comfortable for you or do you feel a need to get away or shut the baby up? Or do you desperately need to soothe, comfort, quiet the baby? What about an older child? Is it OK for babies, but not for an older child to keep crying? Do you hear an inner voice judging that as whining or manipulating? Does that inner voice sometimes leak out in a shaming voice to suppress the child? Do you ever feel a sickening sensation upon recognizing a tone or phrase that sounds like something your own parents would say? This last one never fails to humble me right down to the ground.

It's difficult.

Let's look at theory again. Remember the basic teaching that hurts go in and are stored in the body/psyche. Emotional expression is a natural, built-in mechanism for releasing and healing from the effects of these hurts. Crying is an especially important expression for healing from hurt, loss, or disappointment.

What makes this challenging for us is that *we were taught and have learned to confuse the hurt with the discharge or healing expression of the hurt.* We confuse crying with hurt. There are times, of course, when hurt and crying are simultaneous; for example, a baby is acutely hungry or has a diaper pin sticking him in the bottom. So we check before we rule out physical causes. Most of the time, however, *emotional expression is the healing or release;* the hurt is already in there. Think about a time when you've cried about someone you loved and lost. The loss is in the past; it happened, it's over, and you're still carrying the hurt. The tears are a healing expression and working through of your grief. To try to think about it or to beat yourself up because you haven't gotten over it doesn't change the hurt. Usually it only delays the healing.

So this is what happens. We confuse the hurt with the discharge of the hurt. Having accepted a dull numbing as normal, we avoid the acute pain of feeling, expressing and working through the hurt.

Control Patterns

As parents, we need to be able to recognize control patterns. Anything you do to or for your child to stop his crying is very likely a control pattern. Anything your child does to control or stop her own crying is very likely an internalized control pattern. Once a child learns that crying is upsetting to nearby adults and is discouraged or punished, she quickly learns ways to put a halt to it.

Please note that I'm not talking about the occasional need or desirability of pragmatic distraction or redirection of attention; this is part and parcel of parenting. When it is systematic, however, there is a problem. When there is insufficient time and space to encourage and allow the healing experience of emotional expression, there is a problem. And any mechanism that enforces and ensures the perpetuity of this problem of suppressed emotion is a control pattern.

Control patterns have many faces. Some appear benign: a toy, a joke, a game, or sending the child out to play. Some appear as parent resources: a pacifier, educational programming, a Disney video. Some are recommended disciplinary techniques: "time-out," banishment to the bedroom, loss of a privilege or, on the "positive" side, praises, rewards, gold stars, money, etc. Some appear harsh: spanking and verbal shaming. Some appear under the guise of responsibility and maturity: "big boys don't cry," "use your words," "you can handle that now," "I never saw tears get anything done." It is probably quite obvious to you by now that I view the drugging of hundreds of thousands of children in our society as a mass societal control pattern, and a particularly dangerous one. For adults in our society, we have electroshock as a backup control pattern.

Control patterns range from behaviors that are of themselves loving (feeding, comforting) and benign (joking, distracting) to the outright cruelty of overt physical abuse. The prevalent use of pacifiers for infants and toddlers is a clear example of how far we have gone to suppress our children's feelings. *What possible good is a pacifier other than to promote docility, passivity and quietude in a child meant to express loudly and boisterously much of the time?*

The best approaches I know to handle this problem of control patterns require giving your child time and attention. Be sure to spend your Special Time together *doing what she wants to do.* Rather than always attempting to soothe, distract or punish away your child's crying, move in close and take an interest, listen to and support him in his expression, keep bringing his attention back to the hurt, back to the situation, back to the complaint. *I think this is especially important with boys who by a very early age are already internalizing our societal prohibition on crying for males. It is helpful to slow them down, to gently restrain them from bouncing up, brushing off the hurt and getting back into the game.* Be aware of how well we reward and celebrate our young male athletes for "playing with pain"; be aware of the shame and stigma on those who don't. Most of all, remember to take delight in your child's ability to heal by crying. You have learned that the emotional expression is not the hurt; it is the release of the hurt. The tears are the healing.

I recently received the gift of a poem by my friend Bill Jeffers that I want to share with you now. It conveys the spirit of *The Wildest Colts* wonderfully and illustrates the lesson of control patterns.

DON'T BE NICE
By Bill Jeffers

> Don't be nice.
> Hey, Don't be nice.
> Don't be quiet.
> Never shut up.
> Make a noise, yell, talk real loud.
> Scare everybody.
> Scare yourself.
> Stomp around.
> Want something. Try to get it.

Believe something.
Think a little bit.
Try to be right, think about it.
Think about it.
Be afraid, yes.
Be afraid.
That makes sense.
Feel that.
don't run away.
Be there.
Be that.
Don't be afraid to be afraid.
Want something anyway.
You get to want it.
That's yours at least.
You get to want it.
Go ahead and want it.
Want it for everybody.
That's the trick.
Want it for everybody,
then try to get it, yes!
You get to try to get it.
You can try as long as you want.
It might be hard.
You might have to struggle.
It's alright to struggle.
It doesn't have to be easy.
Don't let go.
Hang on anyway.
Don't turn away.
Be stubborn.
Be a pain in the ass.
Remember that you want it.
Remember why you want it.
Keep trying.
They might think you're crazy.
Do something ridiculous.
Do it anyway.
Do it because.

Do what you want.
Don't listen to anybody.
Be a little different.
You are different.
Scare them.
Go ahead.
Scare yourself.
Be afraid.
You won't die from being afraid.
You can live through being afraid.
They're going to think you're crazy.
You're not crazy.
Just keep wanting.
Just keep thinking.
Make lots of friends.
Get close to everybody.
Be kind to everybody but.
Don't be nice.
Cry when you're hurting.
Yell when you see it.
Make a noise.
Make a big noise.
It's late.
It's as late as it seems.
But don't give up.
You get to keep hoping.
Hang onto your hope.
Don't give that one to them.
If it's gone,
go get it!
Don't be nice.
That belongs to you.
Don't let them have that.
Don't let them have your hope.
They won't take care of it.
It's yours.
Hold it close.
Hold it up high.
Share it.
Don't be nice.

A Good Enough Reason to Cry

Probably all of us have internalized some standard of what is a "good enough" reason to cry. So we respond *very differently* to our child depending on *our judgment* of the situation. If it is a good enough reason (perhaps an obvious physical trauma like a broken leg), we are supportive and understanding. If it's "nothing to cry about" (the proverbial spilt milk), we are impatient, shaming, scolding, admonishing. Most of the time, however, the truth of the matter is that our judgments are irrelevant to the child's needs. Our judgments reflect our distress; they influence us to act in a way that reveals a fundamental distrust of our child's natural intelligence and instincts to work on her needs.

As a parent, your challenge is to extend trust and respect toward your child. The good news is that, in many ways, it really makes your job easier. You are relieved of the onerous burden of judging and evaluating the worthiness of your child's expression. Instead, you only need to keep showing up with good attention, relaxed confidence, and trust that your child will use you as a resource to work things out in the very best way. At the very best, we can only make semi-informed guesses as to the nature of our child's inner reality and what he is working on. Big tears about an *"apparently"* insignificant incident may mean there's something far from insignificant in that experience for her; or it may mean that he's using a trivial incident to counsel on something that happened at school that morning or with a neighbor last week. No matter. Relax, trust and enjoy your child.

Congratulate yourself for being there.

CHAPTER 11
Fear

Whenever I think about fear, Georgia O'Keefe immediately comes to mind. This magnificent artist was quoted as saying, "There was never a day in my life when I wasn't absolutely terrified, but it *never* kept me from doing anything I wanted to do!" What an amazing statement.

There seems to be great confusion in our society about fear. We extol fearlessness, placing great value on the person (generally a man) who "knows no fear." At the same time, we tend to be very fearful and manifest this fear in how we treat our children. *I challenge you to notice how often you say "Be careful" to your child.* Think about it.

Jean Liedloff, in *The Continuum Concept,* gives a wonderful illustration of childrearing in a nature-based tribal society. The children are free to range the edges of steep cliffs and fire pits without concern. They are expected to learn awareness, not caution. In our own society, we teach our children to be afraid. Notice the mailings and late night TV spots depicting lost children. The impression is that children are in great danger of abduction; yet the actual number of abductions is very small and, in fact, more than 90 percent of these so-called "abductions" are committed by parents who have been denied legal custody. The way mass media handles "News" in this country saturates us with fear. Sensationalist journalism takes a horrific incident from anywhere in the state, country or world and brings it into your home and into your mind. You feel as if these daily horrors were happening right next door and you were indeed living in an extremely dangerous neighborhood.

In our confusion about fear, we tend to think that we *should not* be afraid, yet we feel fear. This apparent contradiction leaves us feeling wrong and ashamed. Then we have not only fear to contend with, but also shame. This confused and shame-filled condition is reflected in our parenting. As with crying, we end up making judgments about what is a good enough reason to be afraid. What we judge to be a genuine threat is acceptable: a fierce pit bull dog shows up in your yard, and you comfort your child. A "silly" fear (perhaps seeing an imaginary figure, perhaps falling off an 18-inch high stool, or asking a neighbor for a cup of milk), however, is lightly dismissed, laughed at or scorned.

Fearlessness—living without the feeling of fear—is certainly a wonderful state to experience. Yet we do know fear. Remember that bravery does not mean we act without fear. On the contrary, bravery means we act *in spite of* our fear. Did you know that the word courage is of French derivation and means "big heart"? To be brave requires a big heart. It means you care enough to walk toward and through that which you fear.

We think of fear as a result of our minds living in the future and generate fear when we anticipate or expect bad things to happen. Perhaps you've heard that FEAR is an acronym for Fantasy Expectations Appearing Real. There is some truth in this, and it is reflected in the way we respond to our children's fears. It seems the most common adult reaction to children's fears is to reassure, reinterpret, explain away, logically show why the fear is irrational: "You can't *really* hurt yourself falling 18 inches."; "There really are no ghosts in the closet."; "June bugs *really* don't bite."

One thing most people don't know about fear is that *fear is more an emotional memory of threatening **past*** *experiences than it is about the future.* For example, our intense fear of death comes not so much from our anticipation of dying as it does from our memory of past experiences when we thought and felt that we might die (and, if you believe in reincarnation, where we did die). Our life and death struggle just to be born left a very powerful imprint on us.

Another thing few people know is that fear has more to do with the body than with the mind. *Fear is a tension held in the body* as an unreleased memory of terrifying past experiences. Therefore, it is basically impossible to heal fear by talk. We may distract ourselves and focus our attentions elsewhere, but as with other hurts, healing of fear requires emotional expression. Fear is discharged from the body by shaking, trembling and sweating. Physical pushing is often necessary to unstick and release the frozen energy of fear; squeezing or holding on tight to someone usually helps; screaming often helps, as well.

The best way to help a child release fear is to have a relaxed, confident adult get in close and stay close. Safety, protection and physical closeness are essential to working with a child's fear. As with crying, or any emotion for that matter, our adult judgment about a "good enough" reason is at best irrelevant and at worst downright harmful. Trust your child, be grateful that she is working this out and take pride in the fact that you have made it safe enough for her to counsel on this with you.

Heavy Fears and Light Fears

It is useful to make a distinction between heavy fears and light fears. Much of what I just shared with you is about heavy fear: where a child is really stuck or frozen and just can't move, where you see that look of terror flash on his face. If he shows anger, he needs to push against you. The discharge will be heavy: shaking, trembling, sweating.

Light fears can often be worked with in a light way. They frequently show up as embarrassment. Because the discharge is much lighter, they can often be dissolved by laughter. Use humor, play and silliness; your child will love it. For instance, if your daughter is afraid of climbing on an 18-inch ladder, you can make a great game of this by gently encouraging, celebrating and catching the child again and again. Or *you* climb and *you* fall; make it a big dramatic pratfall. Your child will laugh exuberantly as she watches you fall time after time. Dramatize! Be a ham!

If your son is working on his fear of looking clumsy while playing ball with his friends, make a game of it. *You play and you be excruciatingly embarrassed as you goof up. Let him laugh at you.* This is the key: it is a great service to help your child work on his issues through you.

Help Your Child

We have the erroneous idea in our society that children should be able to work out their peer issues on their own. As always, truth is a double-edged sword: independence and dependence, overprotection and abandonment. It's good to be aware of the need to let your child work things out and have his own experiments, trials and mistakes. At the same time, as parents, we all too often take our child to the park or some other play environment, send her off and expect her to handle what comes up while we take a well-deserved break.

Well, she may handle it very well and she may not. Have you ever expected your child to easily manage an area that is excruciatingly difficult for you, or which you are simply not handling? Observing social interaction on the playground has been good for me, since I have struggled with shyness for some time. I still have a hard time with social play, especially with new people, so it's been a challenge for me to support my children on this issue.

Our children need our help in social situations with their peers. It truly makes sense to be their ally at these times. Play with them and other children. Ask the other children's names, introduce them, initiate some play activity. Expect to be a magnet. Children will gravitate towards you as an adult who pays them attention, enjoys them, plays with them, has fun with them. Your child will love you for it, albeit, perhaps only after she works on her fear, humiliation and rejection by laughing at you, mocking you, acting indifferent, or showing some other behavior.

Be prepared also for this to be very hard at times. Any feelings you still have of embarrassment from past hurts and rejections will likely surface. *Most of us adults have been hurt in such a way that, rather than being sheer joy, play is excruciating.*

LEARNING TO PLAY AGAIN MAY VERY WELL BE THE MOST SIGNIFICANT AND POWERFUL ACTION WE CAN TAKE TO BECOME MORE EFFECTIVE PARENTS, TO GET CLOSER TO OUR CHILDREN AND TO EXPERIENCE GREATER JOY IN OUR LIVES!

It is important that you get support for yourself in learning to play. The Re-Evaluation Counseling Community is a great resource (see Resource Section at end of book). As hard as it is, it really is good news that by helping your child in play, you will help yourself enormously. Active, involved parenting is one of the most powerful and effective ways on the planet to achieve personal growth. *In order to help your child discharge and walk through fear, you must discharge and walk through fear. The best way to counsel your child on an area of distress is to challenge yourself in that same area.*

Take a Risk

Remember Georgia O'Keefe. You have fear, but it is just a feeling memory, an artifact of the past that is largely irrelevant except to indicate a place that needs special attention and healing. Don't let fear stop you. Take strong action and get good support to help you express and release the old hurts as you go along.

I asked you earlier to notice how often you said "Be careful!" or some related admonition like "Watch out!", "Play it safe!", "Don't hurt yourself!" or "Don't fall!" Did you know that children (and our own "inner children") tend not to process negatives? That means that "Don't fall!" becomes "Fall!" "Don't hurt yourself!" becomes "Hurt yourself!" Even more significant is that our energetic communication carries a much greater potency than our words. Frequent admonitions of caution convey your expectation that your child will be hurt or will hurt himself. Such messages tend to become self-fulfilling prophecies as your child tries to oblige you by meeting your expectations.

This point is most especially important with our daughters, since we are apt to cut our sons more slack. Generally speaking, with boys we need to do more protecting, cuddling, pulling them in close. With girls, however, we are required to do the opposite to combat the effects of gender conditioning in our society. *With our daughters, we need to encourage boldness and adventure.*

When your child leaves the house, resist the temptation to advise caution and encourage her to be bold and brave by sending her off with a zesty "Take a Risk!" Replace "Be Careful." with "BE AWARE!" Trust your child's intelligence and judgment. Know that your relaxed confidence will be rewarded as she counsels with you on the issues where it gets hard for her, and as she shares the richness of her life with you. Remind your children that they can play rough and tumble and get hurt and recover completely. Encourage your child to be aware, awake and fully alive.

CHAPTER 12
Anger

Our society also fosters many misconceptions about anger. Because few of us had healthy role models as children, most of us don't have a clue about how to handle anger when it arises in our relationships now, especially within our immediate families. Think about your own parents and how they handled anger. Either it was such a potent force that we were not even allowed to acknowledge its existence, or we became victims of or witnesses to the great harm caused by misdirected and inappropriate anger. Many of us were injured as children by big people expressing the hateful, hurtful energies of their repressed rage. No wonder we are afraid of anger and conditioned to view and experience it as highly dangerous. No wonder we get stuck here with our children.

No wonder that one of the biggest challenges for parents is children's "disrespect." I am convinced that this is the area in which our parenting breaks down the most and where we most unleash our repressed anger on our children. It is one of the hardest problems to see clearly and change and one of the most distressed areas in our society.

A good way to identify patterns of societal distress is to notice when we most strongly experience feelings of shame, judgments and disapproval. And when is this? Most often it is when a child delays, questions, looks defiant, disobeys, talks back, yells back, makes fun of, hits or hits back, or in some other way acts "disrespectfully." These behaviors toward another child are "bad" enough, but when directed toward a parent or other adult evoke incredible feelings of shame, judgments and actions from the adults. Notice where you draw your own "line in the sand" on the ascending, but quite incomplete list of "disrespectful" behaviors that I just provided. Notice your judgments in relationship to yourself and your child. Notice also your judgments in relationship to other parents and their children. There is a treasure here to be uncovered if you are feeling a little bold and adventurous.

Notice what happens inside yourself when you are angry with your child. A basic teaching of Buddhism is that anger comes from blocked desire. When we desire something and our desire is frustrated, we get angry. When we desire and expect a certain behavior or attitude from our child and we don't get it, we get angry. When we desire to be seen by our friends as "good" parents of a "well-mannered" child and our child talks back, we get angry with our child.

Parental Heaven and Hell

There is a Zen story of a pilgrim who approached a master, asking him to reveal the nature of Heaven and Hell. The master, without hesitation, told the pilgrim how gross and stupid he was for asking such a question. The pilgrim was furious. His face became red and grotesquely distorted in rage as he raised his sword to strike the master dead. The master remained calm and without hesitation said, "That's Hell," whereupon the pilgrim was enlightened. His countenance was immediately transformed, and he bowed in deep, heartfelt gratitude. The master responded, "And that is Heaven." I think as parents we all know Hell; it is when we are angry and disgusted with our children, when our sword is raised to give them a "well-deserved" punishment.

Think about what image you hold of a spiritual teacher; perhaps you envision a wise old Zen master or sage, the priest, pastor or minister of your church, perhaps a Gandhi, a Martin Luther King, Jr., or a Mother Teresa. Did you know that your child is one of your greatest spiritual teachers? *There is no such being as a sinful, bad or wicked child. Any such feelings and judgments come from within you; they are from your own past. Parental hell is when you have banished painful feelings into your unconscious and you are projecting them onto your child.* The pilgrim's intense fury was well justified at such an insult; his enlightenment came from the realization that his grotesque "hell" came from within. Your child is your great spiritual teacher because, just as the Zen master, she brings this truth to your attention. You can slay your child with your sword of righteous anger, shame and judgment; or you can step back, count to 10 and resolve to work on your own inner hell. As with the pilgrim, the natural result of transcending this Hell is to enter the kingdom of Heaven. *Parental heaven is when you see your child through the eyes of delight.* Your attitude is one of joy, respect and heartfelt gratitude to be in the presence of such a wonderful being.

You are probably familiar with the often quoted words of Jesus Christ that we must become as little children to enter the Kingdom of Heaven. Do you think he meant that only in reference to quiet, gentle, happy, obedient, well-mannered children? Although we usually interpret this comparison in terms of innocence, trust and being in the present moment, I think two of the greatest virtues children possess are their integrity and authenticity. Yet, how much of our anger is directed toward our children because they are not yet conditioned to be duplicitous, to lie, to be polite even when they are angry, to say "Yes, Sir" when they really don't agree, to smile and say "Thank You" when they don't feel grateful? Jesus impresses me as a man of integrity. Wasn't he crucified by an angry mob for his outspoken civil disobedience? As your great teacher, your child will show you, most vividly, the places where you are inauthentic or out of integrity. A spirited child will force you to either suppress him, or be excruciatingly honest with yourself when your words and deeds, or your words and feelings, are not congruent.

On Desire

The Buddha taught that there was suffering, that suffering came from desire, that Enlightenment, or liberation from suffering, came by letting go of desire. In the West, we come out of a Puritan ethic where desire is frowned upon; our insanely materialistic, consumer-oriented society is a wildly out-of-control caricature, a horrific shadow form of repressed desire.

The messages we give our children about desire, about needs and wants, are incredibly conflicted and confusing. On the one hand, we constantly overwhelm them with gross materialistic excess—the media, the stores, entertainment, Grandma and other relatives, birthdays, holidays. It's crazy. On the other hand, we shame them for being greedy or selfish or "throwing a fit" when they don't get what they want, or more of what they already have.

Non-attachment is, indeed, a core teaching of spiritual development. It is not, however, recommended as a primary focus for child development. This is a place for you to examine your own life as an adult, to figure out your own relationship to this grossly materialistic society. Until you do this, you really don't have a ghost of a chance to provide a healthy home for your child and a healthy example for her to watch. This is Step One.

It makes good sense to protect your children from the relentless onslaught of consumer excess driven by perverted values of mindless greed and short-term profit. At the same time, we are deluded as parents if we think we can provide a glass bubble or pristine flower garden that will obviate the need for our child to struggle through the confusing and hurtful effects of Western Civilization. As with yourself, your child will need to be "in recovery from Western Civilization." He can be in great shape to handle this, however, with you as thoughtful ally.

I think it is harmful and unwise to expect any degree of Buddhist-like non-attachment and equanimity from your young child. I also think it is harmful and unwise to give up, to passively surrender to the relentless forces of the marketplace and permissively allow all manner and amount of nonsensical media and products into your life, your child's life in particular. This is where active parenting can make the difference. I strongly recommend interruption and curtailment of media input (see section on TV). Give thought to food and other consumer activities and exert a positive influence on your child in that area. I urge you to think deeply about established holidays and perhaps discover alternative celebrations. Don't expect to figure it all out or to find a right and wrong way of doing it. Just keep thinking and share your thoughts with others. Include your child in experimenting to learn what works best.

I think it is helpful and wise to *expect your child to passionately desire everything and **more** of everything.* The everythings come and go and are insignificant in any lasting sense. The passionate desire, however, is another story. Passion is to be treasured and celebrated. Passion means the ability to be affected. It is about relatedness, about caring. One of our greatest hurts is the suppression of our caring; it is our nature to deeply care about everyone and everything. ALL LIFE IS SACRED! How can we know this without passion?

Say YES to your child's desire! Frequently say NO to the objects of her desire, but say it lightly, with delight. And don't expect your child to like it.

On Disappointment

I'll give you another key here to put in your parent survival handbook; I think I first heard it put just this way by Dan Jones. You have two choices as a parent: either accept and embrace the fact that you will disappoint your child again and again and again, or go crazy! The nature of being human is to desire. As parents, we are the ones with whom our children work out this inevitable suffering of frustrated desire. It is one of the primary duties in our job description.

Counseling on Needs and Wants

I want now to share a few more principles and techniques that I hope will be helpful. Getting back to anger, remember that frustration is a form of anger and that anger is a basic emotion in the repertoire of our survival nature. Anything that interferes with getting our desires met is experienced as an insult and a threat to our being. Remember that children are completely intelligent, but highly inexperienced. Being in a body on this earth is new, confusing and uncertain. Growing up is challenging and very often extremely frustrating. Remember also the idea of Adultism: adult's world, children's place. Take a close look and be amazed at how often your child is forced to accommodate himself to the needs and whims of adult schedules and demands: going to school, being here and there, doing this and that, none of which probably fits your child's agenda, timing or preference.

I have seven suggestions in counseling your child on desire, frustration and disappointment.

(1) **Make sure your own attention is good;** be relaxed, aware, available. Don't try to counsel your child on this hard stuff when you're tense, angry or in some other way upset.

(2) **Encourage and allow emotional expression.** Remember the hurt (frustration, disappointment) is already there; the expression of the hurt (tantrum, crying) is the release of the hurt. It's healing.

(3) **Keep reaching for your angry child.** There is anger and it needs to be allowed and supported. Know, however, that underneath anger is hurt; fear and sadness are waiting to be shown and released. This is a really tough one. Children work out rejection (and this includes denial or rejection of their desires) by rejecting back; you, of course, are the safest and therefore most likely target. Often a child will say "Go away" or "Leave me alone," and perhaps slam his door and hold it shut to keep you out. There are times when a child needs some space, but such times are less frequent than you might imagine. *Most of the time when your child is angrily rejecting you is when he needs you the most.* We are just beginning to understand that abandonment means much more than rejecting the needs of a child who reaches for food or comfort; abandonment also applies to the child who

actively rejects and pushes you away. *Your daughter may experience abandonment on a very deep level when you accept her rejecting declaration and leave her alone in her distress.* She needs you to push against in order to work this thing out. She badly needs you to remember her true nature, that deep down inside she wants to be completely close to you. She needs you to remember this, to counsel her on her distress and not to confuse it with reality. Keep reaching for your angry child.

SPECIAL NOTE: FOR ADVANCED COUNSELORS ONLY
   Numbers 4, 5 and 6 below get into an area that is powerfully restimulating and needs to be handled with great care and attention.
   Please be sure you have very good support in place before you attempt to counsel your children in this way.

(4) Get help in working with heavy anger. Get good, aware help. Remember to watch out for psychiatric pathologizing of your child's behavior. Working with your child's anger is extremely difficult to do on your own, especially when the child is a bit older (by age 4 or 5). Children are strong and rage lends an unbelievably great deal to one's physical power. Further, there is little so restimulating (bringing up one's own distress, fear, anger, whatever) as your beloved child kicking, screaming, pulling your hair out, etc. It is so important to have good adult allies here. I strongly recommend connecting with the great support and parenting information of the Re-Evaluation Counseling Communities (see Resources at end of book).

(5) **Protect your child from harming self, others, property. Your child needs protection at this time; she needs safety and control. It is your job as parent and counselor to prevent her from hurting herself, you, anyone or anything.** It's called "I know you're angry, keep going, express it, and I'm not going to let you hit me, hurt me, bite me, kick me, pull my hair, tear your brother's face off, break my new lamp, your toy, his model airplane, . . ., etc." Obviously this is easier said than done; the overall approach and attitude is the key. Remember the underlying sweet and cooperative nature of your child; stay relaxed and confident as you help her get this stuff out. That's the ideal; we often can't meet the ideal. We need help and we need to remember that children don't need perfect parents; they need parents who keep thinking and never give up.

So you do your best to provide safety and protect your child, yourself and your property from harm. Yet harm will inevitably come; anger is strong energy and you are not god, neither omnipotent nor omnipresent. My sixth suggestion is extremely important.

(6) **Counsel on fear of getting hurt, getting hit.** This is a big one for many of us. We have been physically hurt; many of us were hit by our parents or others and not allowed to show how much it hurt, to fully discharge and heal. We have been conditioned to "Be careful," to be timid, fearful. Women especially have been conditioned against physical power and active use of their bodies. For most women, a crucial aspect of re-emergence and liberation from internalized sexism is to reclaim physical power. The Re-Evaluation Counseling Communities are one good resource for this work. Women's martial arts can be another great

approach. In any event, the idea is to counsel on anything that keeps you from reaching in for your child, in this case, your angry, physically powerful child. Remember that you can play rough and tumble, get hurt, and recover completely.

(7) Remember that your child *really* doesn't want to hurt you or anyone or anything. I know this is hard to believe in the midst of a full-blown tantrum or rage; nevertheless, it is an absolute truth. It is his distress talking; he's letting it all hang out and he desperately needs your help. He badly needs you to remember his true nature and not confuse his toxic, hateful anger with who he really is.

A big part of parenting is damage control: Gotta do it, never ending job, not much fun. Once the damage is done, it's usually too late to effectively counsel the wrongdoer. Once big brother clobbers his little sister, it's the sister who gets support. Even if we do manage not to shame brother too heavily, it's still very hard to counsel him—not just because of our anger or disappointment or overwhelm as parents, but because he will be highly defensive. He feels so bad deep down that he does anything and everything to protect against this feeling—more defiance, indifference, withdrawal, shut down, refusal to talk, guilt, you name it. *A key to effective counseling is to interrupt the hurtful pattern just before the actual hurt.* If you can catch him just before he clobbers sister, you're in great shape to work on this together. Then you stay in close and really pay attention. You let him know that you know he really doesn't want to hurt his sister. You encourage his expression. You may keep him just at arm's length as he tries to kill sister, or he may turn on you. You let him know that you're not going to let him hurt you. (If he gets in a punch and you have to stop, that's OK. You'll get another chance, and this is the kind of work where we really do need help. *In fact, I don't recommend you do this until you feel really strong in counseling your child on crying and fear, and until you've reclaimed the ability to play and are having some good, close, affectionate time with your child. I also strongly recommend getting help.)* As you remind him that you know he really doesn't want to hurt you, he may respond with a screaming "Yes I do! I want to tear your @#*#!@ face off!" Then you can give yourself an internal pat on the back for your good counseling! It's true; this heavy stuff looks awful and can be extremely hard, but it's such a gift to help a child get this out safely.

Often times, your child will move from rage into fear. I'm not talking about the light fears discharged through play; I'm talking about terror, heavy fear. Refer back to the previous chapter for advice on how to work with fear. Remember that the most important factor in helping a child release fear is to have a relaxed, confident adult who gets in close and stays close.

A Note on Restraint

In reading this chapter on anger, I'm sure you have noticed the cautionary emphasis about doing such intense work with your child. Permissive counseling is when you lend support and encouragement to a child who is hurting and who overtly wants your attention— holding a child in your lap while she cries or tells you about being afraid of the dark. Non-permissive counseling, however, is another story. The child is hurting, but she is telling you to go away and leave her alone. Non-permissive counseling is based on the premise that a child really needs and wants your attention even when overtly saying she doesn't. Her overt rejection of your attention when she is hurting is usually an expression of distress; she really needs your help at this time.

This book is about challenging the oppression and control of children. The concept of non-permissive counseling can easily be used as a tool for control or punishment. It requires great awareness and sensitivity to avoid falling into this pit. Especially examine your motives and actions when you feel tense or irritable; *remember that the attitudes of relaxed confidence and loving delight are the best indicators of a good time to counsel your child.*

I must acknowledge that it feels strange to emphasize caution; after all, I have throughout this book advised you to encourage your children to be bold and to take risks. I also encourage you to take risks in your parenting. Remember that children don't need perfect parents and that they are robust. The keys are to stay awake and aware, keep thinking and get lots of support.

With all this in mind, I now directly address the concept of restraint—holding a child, preventing his leaving, or his striking out at someone or something. Non-permissive by nature, restraint is a primary tool of coercive authority. Police do it, soldiers do it, psychiatrists do it. Restraint is historically, and still today, mostly a practice of authoritarian control. It easily serves that purpose with children. I feel like I could go on and on. What I want to make clear is that restraint can also be used with awareness and thoughtfulness to help a child release hurt and pain. In fact, I would go so far as to say that restraint is at times a necessary technique for helping a child deal with heavy fear and anger. My advice about using restraint is as follows:

(1) **Make sure your attention is good**—aware, thoughtful, relaxed, confident, loving—before you attempt to counsel your child on strong feelings.

(2) **Get as much help and support as possible** from other aware adults.

(3) **First try to exhaust permissive counseling strategies**—talking, gentle attention, playfulness, expressions of concern, invitations to closeness, approaching the child, light touch, etc.

(4) **Remember the inherent nature of your child**— that she is intelligent, cooperative and loving, and, underneath the distress, wants to be completely close and affectionate with you.

(5) **Monitor your own emotions and attitudes**—if at all possible, avoid counseling your child when you are tense, angry, needy or otherwise emotionally stimulated.

(6) **Use the minimum amount of restraint required** to ensure safety and to facilitate emotional expression. Holding a child too rigidly usually results in a shutdown of expression. **Allow as much movement as possible within your protective holding**—active struggle is usually most helpful in facilitating your child's emotional discharge.

Beyond Words

I have one last, most important point to make about this type of work with children; it is WAY BEYOND WORDS. I am writing in an attempt to provide a mental explanation of an intense physical and emotional experience, an experience to which we all bring loads of conflicting feelings and values. You will not learn to do this work effectively by reading this book. My final advice for those of you who want to try this approach is this:

*Find and participate with other adults who are doing
this work. Let them be models for you and support you in
counseling on the feelings that such intense conflict and
emotional discharge bring up for you.*

The play groups and family workshops of the Re-
Evaluation Counseling Community are the best places I
know of to learn and practice counseling children.

CHAPTER 13
About Eric

I had a very hard time with my son, Eric, when he was between the ages of 4 and 7. He was angry a lot, demanded a lot of attention, and was seldom content or satisfied. As a father, I was taxed to my limits again and again, especially by his anger, defiance and obstinancy. A session might begin when I would interrupt his attempt to hit his little sister or throw a toy or other object. When I stayed close and did not accept his rejection or allow him to isolate into his room or run away outside, he would turn his fury on me and hit me or pull my hair. I would do my best to thoughtfully restrain him, but I inevitably took some shots. I had some fear of him, but I think my biggest fear was about him—that he would never get through this, that he was and would be "emotionally disturbed," that we were creating a monster.

I was furious with him. There were times when I felt like killing him. By the grace of God, I never struck out at him, but I have to admit that there was a time or two when I was overzealous in restraining him during a session. I yelled at him more than I like to admit. In retrospect, this is what I think happened.

His mother and I made Eric go to pre-school/day care when he clearly didn't want to. Many times over he furiously resisted as I carried him to the car and strapped him into his carseat. Part of the difficulty was probably his parents' insecurity about being separated from him. I am sure, however, that an even greater part was Eric's spirited fight for what he wanted and knew was best for him—to stay home! We finally accepted that and he has thrived. Only this year, at age 9, is Eric back in school and doing great! I am convinced that Eric would have been considered an ideal candidate for psychiatric labeling and drugging. Now his teacher considers him a model of good attention for the other students!

But as I take a deeper look at the struggle we went through, I am convinced that my own difficulty with anger was a big factor. My anger was suppressed; I was a "passive passive" in many ways. I would sacrifice my own needs and withdraw from conflict. I have no doubt that Eric was picking up on and expressing my anger as well as his own. Children do that.

It's also true that Eric was born angry. Though born at home with loving support and without drugs, his birth was hard. He had a big head and was stuck in hard labor for several hours. When he finally emerged, he was wide awake, aware and alert, and he looked intense, as if he'd been through a fight—which he had. Then he and his mother had difficulty getting the nursing established for a day, and Eric raged and raged. What a relief when they finally got that handled!

We were learning. Our daughter, Vanessa, had a much easier birth. She also got the benefit of the experience we had gained with Eric. Typically, we spent a great deal more time in the attitude of "relaxed confidence" in Vanessa's earliest years than we had in Eric's.

We were exposed to and learning good counseling theory as we went along with Eric. We liked what we saw and heard. It made good sense, but we were like a pilot program. We heard about people who allowed children to "be the boss," to be "disrespectful" and "out-of-control," but we had no real, live models to follow. It was very hard to trust that our wild child, easily diagnosable by mental health professionals as some kind of "disruptive behavior disorder," would turn out loving, cooperative, sweet, sensitive and powerful in a good way. Now I can tell you in all truth and sincerity that this is exactly how I would describe my son, Eric. He is still a pistol and still challenging, and *he is such a joy!*

But when he was angry, for so long and with such intensity, I often felt overwhelmed. As we counseled him during his angry sessions by physically restraining him, we began to see the fear flash on his face. He would start to panic and say we were hurting him. He would have difficulty breathing and begin to choke. It eventually became clear to me that he was working on his birth trauma. Fortunately I had a lot of experience counseling adults on birth trauma, so I could see this and accept it. Even so, *I promise you that counseling an aware and cooperative adult is very different from counseling your own panicky child* who is fighting you and projecting the whole experience onto you (blaming you). It was so hard. We had a lot of help or we wouldn't have been able to work with Eric the way we did.

I want to share with you one more amazing phenomenon that kept surfacing in my work with Eric and continues today. Although it seemed that much of the time Eric was incredibly angry and difficult, the truth is his "big" sessions really only occupied a small percentage of his life. At the "worst" times, I'm sure that no more than 10 percent of the time was he directly confrontive and challenging. Even this amount was largely due to our inexperience and uncertainty as parents in effectively responding to and counseling him well. I know I have observed this same phenomenon in other parents.

As difficult as Eric's emotional distress was to handle, it is ironic that his natural, undistressed state was really my greatest challenge! This is hard to admit, but I believe it's true. So much of the time, I felt (and honestly still do to some degree) that the only time I could be with Eric in a relaxed and comfortable way was when he was sick. (This was especially true when I was suffering through an extended illness of my own, but it was generally true at all times.) Eric's naturally robust energy, zest and power is incredible; he simply felt like way too much for me to handle. From these experiences has come the realization and acceptance of the profound but uncomfortable truth:

Much of the suppression we do to our children is not in response to the hurts they show us; the greater part (and this definitely includes the drugging of our children) is our pathetic attempt to control, slow down, rein in their dynamic aliveness!

But I haven't yet told you the most amazing part of all this—the realization that possibly I am just like my son and that, as a child, I may have been as robust, zestful, challenging, energetic and alive as he is now. I have noticed this phenomenon in other parents as well. For example, I have a friend who has long believed that she is very much like her son, but very different from her daughter. It is her relationship with her daughter (like mine with Eric) that's most challenging, however; this is where the emotional intensity lies and where the sparks tend to fly. Of special interest is the fact that as my friend is currently experiencing a major phase in her own personal growth, she has spontaneously awoken to the possibility that she really is quite like her daughter. The difference was that this woman's challenging, robust aliveness had been so effectively suppressed as a child that it seemed completely foreign and not a part of her true nature. This is how it was for Eric and me. I still don't know how much like Eric I am. I do know that the very idea has been extremely useful in my own personal counseling and that recovering my own emotional energy has helped me relate to my son more effectively.

Please get all the help you can. I am convinced that the years of intensive parenting were a major factor in my eventual divorce from Eric and Vanessa's mother. Don't expect to do this really intense level of work without good, strong support. Remember through it all to see yourself and your partner and your child with as much compassion as you can possibly bring to bear. You all deserve it!

CHAPTER 14
Four Techniques

I have said much about counseling theory and about various faces of emotional distress. This chapter offers four techniques that will help to bring this theory to life for you.

(1) The Three Times (3X) Rule

I learned this one by experience with my son, Eric. There was a long period when he was often unhappy. I really tried to accommodate him, honor his desires, "correct for" the apparent rigidity in my own upbringing. Food and eating was a focal point where we worked this one out. I would prepare something for Eric, often something he had requested, but then I served it on the "wrong" plate, cut it up "wrong," or poured the syrup "wrong," or whatever. The same phenomenon could happen with this toy or that toy, or this T-shirt or that underwear.

It took me quite awhile, but I eventually learned to discern whether or not Eric was expressing a genuine desire. I wanted to honor his preferences and not impose my own tastes or conditions on him. What I learned was that oftentimes Eric's want, need or desire was unrelated to food or clothing or whatever the apparent task at hand. I say "apparent" most deliberately because it became quite clear that no matter what I did or gave, no matter how I accommodated him, he was still angry and unsatisfied. Remember what I said earlier about disappointment; Eric was going to be disappointed no matter what I did.

So eventually it dawned on me that *Eric was clearly showing his real need at these times, which was to coun-*

sel on his disappointment and dissatisfaction, or to counsel on his felt rejections by actively rejecting whatever I might do for him.

This was an extremely helpful insight for me, and I learned that I could use this 3x phenomenon as a rule of thumb. It works like this. If I accommodate him three times and he is *still* griping, moaning, complaining, or verbally insulting me, then there's a very good chance this has little or nothing to do with food or clothes. If you are responsive to your child's expressed wishes and he is still out of sorts and upset with you, then he is probably asking for, demanding, a counseling session. I use the 3x rule as a guide, especially when my own intuition is not very strong.

At this point, it is better not to accommodate. It is the time to clearly say no and, with relaxed confidence, counsel your child by listening to her complaints, encouraging her expression, acknowledging how hard and frustrating it is, or how greatly disappointed she is. If your attention is good, this is a great time to counsel your child because her distress is just right there and she is showing you how hard it is.

(2) Encouraging Your Child's Desire

This is an excellent technique to use at the above juncture when you give a clear NO to your child's further requests or in general when you are clear and relaxed about a refusal of what your child wants. Remember what I said before; the direction is called Say YES to your child's desire while saying NO to the object of her desire. It's called "No, Darling we're not buying that new toy, but I can see you *really* want it." This is the opposite of suppressing your child and making her wrong for wanting things so bad, judging her or trying to socialize her out of being greedy, selfish, or materialistic. The idea is to encourage her to express how badly she wants it, how frustrated and disappointed she is that she can't have it because you won't buy it for her. Do not expect her to sympathize with your financial concerns! When you counsel this way, a key is not to distract your child so she won't think or feel about the desired object. This may be a useful ploy to get out of the store, but it is not counseling on the distress. *Rather than distract, you keep gently bringing your child's attention back to her desire.* Say things such as, "You really want that doll, don't you!" or "I'm sorry you can't have that toy you really want!" or "I know how much you want that neon telephone." Sometimes, it is most helpful just to place a hand between your child and the desired object. You let her want it, allow and encourage her reaching while you gently hold her back, just out of reach. There are times when a child will very effectively get her frustration out this way.

So you encourage her expression, her greed, her lust, her dramatic heart-breaking suffering at not getting that neon telephone! Remember that it's really not about the neon telephone. She's working out her desire and frustration. Counseling her this way will help her find a rational ground on which to stand in the midst of a society that so mindlessly drifts on the polluted waters of crass materialism!

(3) Role Reversal

This means you play the child. This useful and versatile technique is best used when you sense that you can handle your child's unmet desires with lightness. If your child is expressing heavy feelings, encourage that. But if the feelings are not so intense, you can try having fun with the situation. Be like a child; play with it. For example, say "I want it! It's mine!" "No, it's mine!" "No, you can't have it. MINE!" Wrestle over it. Have fun with it. Be greedy. Be silly.

This can also mean that the child plays you, or a teacher or other authority with whom she is displeased. It means encouraging your child to imitate, make fun of or otherwise get into the character who is denying her desires. It will likely mean that you allow and encourage a most "disrespectful" attitude toward authority on the part of your child. Remember that this is counseling to release emotional distress; it is *not* about the moral education of your child. It can actually be great fun and can result in tremendous lightening up of the situation for your child.

(4) Dramatized Grievances

Encouraging your child to dramatize his anger when he feels wronged is very helpful. Let's say his teacher has acted unjustly; he is furious and he wants revenge. He wants to kill her. As individuals, our tendency is to be afraid of such intense rage and do whatever we can to discourage its expression. Particularly as parents, we are strongly affected when we see the face of unsocialized aggression in our sweet child. We may be afraid, ashamed, or appalled and aghast. We may react with our own rage. Certainly we are concerned.

This technique of dramatizing a grievance is a way to work with clearing and releasing your child's emotional energy. No judgment is necessary. For future reference, as your child's ally, you may wish to discern whether or not your child's grievance is part of an ongoing situation with which she needs help. For the purpose of this counseling moment, however, your judgments about the rightness of her rage are irrelevant. Something big is up for her and she needs to get it out. A dramatized grievance means to dramatize the grievance. Act it out. Exaggerate it. Really get into it. If she wants to kill the teacher, encourage her to go into how and include the grisly details. Remember, however, that this is not your rage, your drama, so watch out about "stealing your child's thunder." Relax. Remember your child's true loving and cooperative nature. Trust that expressing feelings, even rage, in a safe and appropriate way (with you and not by stabbing the teacher or vandalizing the classroom) will not lead your child to a homicidal future. Emotional release in the presence of a loving, supportive ally/parent will do the opposite, in fact, by helping restore your child to her natural zest and intelligence.

Addendum to Technique: Reminders of Inherent Reality

These techniques can be very powerful. Better said, the distressing feelings which the techniques help release are often extremely intense. The feelings distort perception and promote confusion; residual thoughts related to hurt or revenge can remain. It is very important to spend a little time with your child talking about the experience, fishing for the unclear residue or misperception that it is his fault. After a session, ask your child how he views the situation and the people involved. This is a great time to counteract two huge oppressions of children. One is inadequate information; use the opportunity to encourage the understanding that people are always inherently good, but act in hurtful ways as a result of carrying unreleased distress from their own past hurts. Two is disrespect; disrespect leads to internalized shame, the feeling that comes from a message that the child is to blame for being treated badly. Here is an opportunity to contradict this feeling by letting your child know that there is never *any* reason for him to be treated badly and without respect. Remind him once again of his inherent goodness and lovability, and enjoy once more the vision of your child through the Eyes of Delight!

CHAPTER 15
Sharings From Two Women Leaders

The Work of Patty Wipfler

One of my main teachers on parenting is Patty Wipfler. Patty is International Reference Person on Parenting for the Re-Evaluation Counseling Communities. She has also published a number of outstanding written resources through the Parents Leadership Institute. Please read Appendix A. It is a long excerpt from one of Patty's booklets entitled *Listening to Parents.* The excerpt is a wonderful summary of the healing process of emotional discharge. Carefully read her description of the process in children; continue on and get a glimpse of how using "listening partnerships with fellow parents" can help us in our own healing!

The Appendix also includes information on how to order the resource materials Patty Wipfler has created. *I cannot recommend highly enough that you avail yourself of this great information.*

The Spoiled Family Outing

Below is one more item from Patty Wipfler's work, an excerpt from her booklet on "Crying." Patty describes a phenomenon that is a huge, ongoing challenge and is like a rite of passage into parenthood. It has to do with the fact that, to quote Patty, "Happy Times Often Bring Up Unfinished Griefs."

As if to make parenting even more of a test of character, children often choose happy, close times with you to bring up feelings of upset. I call this the "spoiled outing" phenomenon. You have just spent a happy day with your children, perhaps at the park or with their cousins, playing and doing the things they love. As you head for home, your children become unhappy and easily upset. They cry about having to sit in the back seat, over your request that each child carry his own jacket, or because you've stopped at McDonalds, not Burger King. A parent's mood at moments like these tends to be grim. "If this is how you act, I'm not bringing you to the park again!"

What the children are actually doing is taking advantage of the extra feelings of safety and closeness they have gathered throughout the day. The backdrop of a day's satisfaction makes the imperfections in life stand out, like spaghetti stains on a white tablecloth. Because he's had such a happy day, your child now turns to address sadness he still carries. For your child, this is an efficient way to flush out stored upsets. If you don't expect it, however, a "spoiled outing" can be frustrating or even infuriating. Once you realize that it happens like clockwork you are in a much better position to listen as your child cries his upsets into peace of mind. For instance, you can begin to head for home before all your energy is spent, knowing that along the way there will be some constructive falling apart to be done.

Words From Diane Shisk

I close Part III of this book, On Counseling Children, by sharing with you a little list provided by Diane Shisk, another international leader in the Re-Evaluation Counseling Community. It is taken from the October 1995 issue of Present Time, the Journal of the Re-Evaluation Counseling Communities. I think it is a wonderful summary of this work and a great guide to communicating with your children.

Beloved Child, You Are Wanted

Here are some things to communicate to your children everyday, in your own words, and in ways that communicate from you to them:

You are wanted. I am very happy to have you in my life. I want you to be close with me forever.

I love you. I will always love you. Nothing will ever stop me from loving you.

You can make a difference in any situation.

Your feelings are important. I want to know how you feel, no matter what the feelings are.

You are unique and special. No one else is you. You are precious in who you are. You don't have to be like anyone else.

All people are alike in being intelligent, loving, cooperative, creative, and human. The world has many, many people, each as precious as you and me.

You are strong and growing stronger. You can play rough and tumble, get hurt, and recover completely.

I may have to leave you for a short time, but I will always return. If something should happen and I get lost for a while, I will fight my way back to you.

You matter. You are important because you are you.

You can have lots of friends. Many people will want to know you and want you to know them. You can make a friend of anyone you choose.

You can learn anything. There's no problem you can't solve or skill you can't master. You are very smart.

You never have to be alone. You can be completely close to many people and keep them close always.

You never have to give up or stop trying on anything. You can go after your biggest dreams. No one can ever make you give up.

Trust your thinking. Listen to others and share your thinking with them. Ask questions, get all the information you need, and decide what is true and right.

You can make your own choices. You get to live the life you choose for yourself. Other people will make different choices for themselves; you get to make your own for you.

No person ever deserves to be mistreated or ignored. People only treat each other badly because they have been hurt and not listened to.

There are many problems to be solved. Many people are hurt and unable to treat each other well. But many people are thinking about what should be done to fix things and are joining together to make things right. We will be able to set everything right, and you will be able to help us.

Appendix A

An Introduction to Patty Wipfler's Work

(Taken from *Listening to Parents,* pp. 15 - 20)

A Summary of Emotional Healing and Listening Partnerships

To explain this healing process, we shall begin by talking about the lives of children, because children are real experts at healing from upset feelings. We also refer to childhood because, if you are like most people, you will find as you talk in your sessions that many of the tensions you now battle have their roots in your early years, when you were most easily hurt.

People are naturally trusting, loving, cooperative and eager for challenges.

Do you remember how toddlers tend to approach their lives? They are ready for adventure the moment they wake up in the morning. They trust you and the other people they know, offering friendship and fun to anyone who will play with them thoughtfully. They have boundless energy. Nothing daunts them. They can fall hundreds of times as they learn to walk and run, but they never even think of giving up. When you sweep the kitchen floor, they are right there, eager to do this important work. After they've pushed the broom around with great concentration, they are proud of themselves for a job well done. Their faith in their own goodness is strong. Their delight in life is enormous. Your confidence and pride in yourself was once this complete.

Every hurt hits a young child hard.

The minute you scold a toddler, it's as if his world has caved in. He might look stricken for a second, then burst out crying. Or if you get irritated and try to take his broom away, he might throw himself on the ground in a stormy tantrum. When he is sunny and confident, there are few people who are more aware and alive than a toddler. When he feels hurt, there are few people more completely unhappy. Even small incidents of hurt are deeply felt, and can leave a lasting effect on a child. You probably remember how thoroughly hurt you felt at times when you were young. When you were a child, many incidents of hurt hit you hard.

Children blame themselves for the hurts they suffer.

When children get hurt by thoughtlessness, mistreatment or circumstance, they are saddled with emotional tension caused by the hurt. A hurtful experience, no matter how insignificant it may seem to an adult, always makes a child feel bad about himself. Children interpret the incidents that hurt them in a thoroughly personal way. They assume that the troubles that befall them are a sign that there is something very wrong with them.

Hence, when a child is made fun of by a jealous sibling, the child can't see that he is being hurt because his sibling is full of tension. He believes he is being called names because something about him really is "stupid," "dumb" or "bratty." Every time a child feels hurt, he internalizes a strong impression that something is wrong with him. This impression causes his behavior to lose flexibility, much like a pebble in your shoe hampers your stride as you walk.

You, too, will tend to blame yourself for your difficulties. You have been hurt through no fault of your own. However, because your troubles have endured, you are pulled to believe that your bad feelings and inability to think are "just the way you are."

155

Unhealed hurts leave scars in the form of rigid, irrational behavior.

Every hurt that goes unresolved robs the child of some of his wonderfully flexible, inventive intelligence. For example, instead of resuming play with his brother, the child who was called names might withdraw from him or become consistently aggressive in his own defense. The child will lose his ability to notice the times when his brother is relaxed and able to play well with him. The stored hurts cut the child's behavior options down to one or two set approaches. They block his ability to understand the nuances of the present situation. Instead of learning, he is set up to react in a stereotyped way, because of the unhealed hurt of earlier incidents.

Children naturally know how to heal from a hurt.

If a child has a parent who will stop, listen and stay close when things go wrong, he will do his best to shed the bad feelings he is saddled with. He will cry if he is sad, tremble and perspire and struggle if he has been frightened, have a tantrum if he is frustrated, laugh away his light fears and embarrassments, and yawn to release physical tension. As these somewhat messy and time-consuming activities take place, the hurtful impression left by the incident (for example, "What you want is unimportant," "You are too much trouble," "Brother can't stand you") is gradually erased from the child's experience. If he is allowed to cry, tremble, and storm all the way through the upset, his full confidence and pleasure in himself will return. When he is finished, he sees the hurtful incident as a harmless glitch in his life, not as a permanent setback.

For example, I know two brothers who were two and four when they decided to race each other. Their mother was outside too, playing attentively with them. The older brother won the first race, and the mother cheered for him, and then embraced the younger son, telling him that he had run very well. They raced again, and this time, the younger son won. The mother came over and hugged him with warm congratulations for coming in first. He turned to her and burst into tears, saying "No! No! No, Mommy!" The mother continued to hold him, mystified by his outburst. She didn't understand what he meant by "No!" so she listened and told him now and then that she was glad he came in first. Finally, he looked at her and said, "No, I'm second! Tommy is first, and I'm second!" He continued to cry hard, while she repeated a few more times that he had come in first, and that his brother had been second. After 15 minutes, he stopped crying, relaxed with her a minute, and asked, "Was I first?" When his mother answered "Yes," he went off serenely to play.

What had happened? Over time, the younger child had internalized the rigid impression that he was always second, and carried some sadness about his supposed limitation. When he won the race and his mother was delighted, the feelings of hurt behind this rigid impression were contradicted, or counterbalanced, by the reality of coming in first. He cried hard, because his put-down of himself could no longer exist side-by-side with his clear victory. Strong feelings were shed and the hurt was lifted. He was then able to gain the fresh understanding that he, the second child, could actually be "first." This is how the healing process works.

Like children, when adults laugh, cry, tremble and perspire, have a tantrum, or yawn while they talk about their troubles, they are relieved of the tensions associated with those hurts.

Their ability to think and act more flexibly is restored. They become more reasonable, more fun-loving, more sure that they are good people, inside and out.

The healing process is often interrupted.

Under most circumstances, adults rarely find enough safety to use this simple, powerful healing process. Most of us had parents who thought that it was their responsibility to stop our deeply felt emotions, or who looked upon this healing process as "misbehavior." We had to learn to stop ourselves from crying, having tantrums, and showing our fear. With no chance to shed feelings of upset, we had greater and greater difficulty recovering our self-respect and enthusiasm for life each time we were hurt.

Although you don't often see adults making use of it, this healing process is natural. Every child is born knowing how to use it. Every infant assumes that her parents will listen with care while she cries through her upsets at the end of each challenging day. The listening partnership is an environment in which an adult can relearn the use of this natural process, and put it to work to resolve the tensions that interfere with loving, playing, learning, and taking full charge of life.

Listening gets this healing process started.

The listening partnership creates a framework in which, much of the time, this healing process begins by itself. Simple, respectful listening, over a period of time, allows a person to come to trust the listener. This trust gradually allows the client to loosen the tight control she has had to keep over her tears, trembling, and laughter. To get the healing process started, simply keep your attention on your listening partner in a friendly and persistent way, session after listening session. *Your attitudes of love, respect, affection, hope, delight, and confidence toward your client will powerfully contradict the impressions left by the hurtful experiences in her life.* For example, with you there letting her know she's good and courageous, your client won't be able to blindly assume that she is a timid person. She can perspire and laugh as she makes plans to speak up for the first time at the upcoming parent meeting at her child's school. With you telling him confidently that he is a loving father, your client might at first laugh in disbelief, but soon begin to cry because he trusts you, and you have brought into question his rigid conviction that he is entirely to blame for his child's difficulties.

To repeat: the attitudes an attentive counselor adopts toward the client are a powerful force in a listening partnership session. These attitudes, consistently held over time, provide the client with the support she lacked when she was first hit by hurt. As she talks about her difficulties now, your attention fills an unmet need. The healing process that was interrupted for lack of a committed listener many years ago can now proceed at last.

This process of tension release takes time, but it is very dependable. With enough release of emotional tension, adults can transform their approach and attitudes in life very thoroughly, from the inside out. They can overcome irrationalities that have burdened them since their early years. After several listening sessions, you will probably find that, now and again, your listening partner has begun to laugh, tremble and perspire, tantrum, cry, or yawn. The healing process is shifting into gear.

How To Order These Resources

Write or call and ask for ordering information on Patty Wipfler's booklets for parents at the following address:

Parents Leadership Institute
P.O. Box 50492
Palo Alto, CA 94303
(415) 424-8687

Appendix B

All About Children: Selected Quotations

Contributed by Leonard Roy Frank

Children have never been very good at listening to their elders, but they have never failed to imitate them.
> JAMES BALDWIN, *Nobody Knows My Name: More Notes of a Native* Son, 3, 1961

It's frightening to think that you mark your children merely by being yourself.
> SIMONE de BEAUVOIR, *Les Belles Images, 3,* 1966, tr. Patrick O'Brian, 1968

The mother's heart is the child's schoolroom.
> HENRY WARD BEECHER, "The Family," *Proverbs from Plymouth Pulpit,* ed. William Drysdale, 1887

[In April 1950, a "mute and autistic" 34^{1}/$_{2}$-month-old boy was administered 20 ECTs after being referred to the children's ward of New York's Bellevue Hospital. A month later he was discharged.] The discharge note indicated "moderate improvement, since he was eating and sleeping better, was more friendly with the other children, and he was toilet trained."
> LAURETTA BENDER, "The Development of a Schizophrenic Child Treated with Electric Convulsions at Three Years of Age," in Gerald Caplan, ed., *Emotional Problems of Early Childhood,* 1955

We are now conducting a sort of general warfare against children, who are being abandoned, abused, aborted, drugged, bombed, neglected, poorly raised, poorly fed, poorly taught, and poorly disciplined. Many of them will not only find no worthy work, but no work of any kind. All of them will inherit a diminished, diseased, and poisoned world. We will visit upon them not only our sins but also our debts. We have set before them thousands of examples – governmental, industrial, and recreational – suggesting that the violent way is the best way. And we have the hypocrisy to be surprised and troubled when they carry guns and use them.
> WENDELL BERRY, "The Obligation of Care," *Sierra,* September-October 1995

Tew bring up a child in the wa he should go – travel that wa yourself.
JOSH BILLINGS, *His Sayings,* 78, 1867

I'm starting to wonder what my folks were up to at my age that makes them so doggoned suspicious of me all the time!
MARGARET BLAIR, in Leonard Louis Levinson, ed., *Bartlett's Unfamiliar Quotations,* p. 336, 1971

Fathers and mothers have lost the idea that the highest aspiration they might have for their children is for them to be wise – as priests, prophets or philosophers are wise. Specialized competence and success are all that they can imagine.
ALLAN BLOOM, "The Clean Slate," *The Closing of the American Mind: How Higher Education Has Failed Democracy and Impoverished the Souls of Today's Students,* 1987

Dr. [Paula] Menyuk and her co-workers [at Boston University's School of Education] found that parents who supplied babies with a steady stream of information were not necessarily helpful. Rather, early, rich language skills were more likely to develop when parents provided lots of opportunities for their infants and toddlers to "talk" and when parents listened and responded to the babies' communications.
JANE E. BRODY, "Talking to the Baby: Some Expert Advice," *New York Times,* 5 May 1987

"Teachers"... treat students neither coercively nor instrumentally but as joint seekers of truth and of mutual actualization. They help students define moral values not by imposing their own moralities on them but by positing situations that pose hard moral choices and then encouraging conflict and debate. They seek to help students rise to higher stages of moral reasoning and hence to higher levels of principled judgment.
JAMES MacGREGOR BURNS, *Leadership,* 17, 1978

Ah! happy years! once more who would not be a boy?
　　LORD BYRON, *Childe Harold's Pilgrimage,* 2.23, 1812-1818

A child. . . opens and closes like a blossom.
　　ELIAS CANETTI, 1978, *The Secret Heart of the Clock: Notes,*
　　Aphorisms, Fragments: 1973-1985, tr. Joel Agee, 1989

Education should be constructed on two bases: morality and pru-
dence. Morality in order to assist virtue, and prudence in order to
defend you against the vices of others. In tipping the scales toward
morality, you merely produce dupes and martyrs. In tipping it the
other way, you produce egotistical schemers.
　　CHAMFORT (1741-1794), *Maxims and Thoughts,* 5, 1796, tr. W. S.
　　Merwin, 1984

While you were a child, I endeavored to form your heart habitually to
virtue and honor, before your understanding was capable of showing
you their beauty and utility.
　　LORD CHESTERFIELD, letter to his son, 3 November 1749

Birth is much, but breeding's more.
　　JOHN CLARKE, ed., *Proverbs: English and Latine,* p. 103, 1639

It [is] very unfair to influence a child's mind by inculcating any
opinions before it [has] come to years of discretion to choose for itself.
　　SAMUEL TAYLOR COLERIDGE (1772-1834), in Tryon Edwards et al.,
　　eds., *The New Dictionary of Thoughts,* p. 156, 1891-1955

A youth is to be regarded with respect.
　　CONFUCIUS (551-479 B.C.), *Confucian Analects,* 9.22, tr. James
　　Legge, 1930

A belief constantly inculcated during the early years of life, while the
brain is impressible, appears to acquire almost the nature of an

*instinct; and the very essence of an instinct is that it is followed inde-
pendently of reason.*
CHARLES DARWIN, *The Descent of Man and Selection in Relation
to Sex,* 2nd ed., 4, 1874

*What we found in examining diaries, letters, autobiographies, pedi-
atric and pedagogical literature back to antiquity was that good parenting appears to be something only historically achieved, and that
the further one goes back into the past the more likely one would be to
find children killed, abandoned, beaten, terrorized and sexually
abused by adults. Indeed, it soon appeared likely that a good mother,
one who was reasonably devoted to her child and more or less able to
empathize with and fulfill its needs, was nowhere to be found prior to
modern times. It seemed to me that childhood was one long night-
mare from which we have only gradually and only recently begun to
awaken.*
LLOYD deMAUSE, "Psychohistory and Psychotherapy,"
Foundations of Psychohistory, 1992

*When you arrange parenting modes on a scale of decreasing health,
from empathic down to the most destructive child-battering parents,
you have also listed historical modes of child care reaching back into
the past. It is as though today's child abuser were a sort of "evolution-
ary arrest," a psychological fossil, stuck in a personality mode from a
previous historical epoch when everyone used to batter children.*
Ibid.

*The certainty with which the effective prohibition of incest has been
declared leads one to look for the evidence these authors might have
for their assertions. Yet such a search soon proves quite fruitless. . .
consider the evidence for the opposite hypothesis: That it is incest
itself—and not the absence of incest—that has been universal for most
people in most places at most times. Furthermore, the earlier in history one searches, the more evidence there is of universal incest, just*

as there is more evidence of other forms of child abuse.
LLOYD deMAUSE, "Universality of Incest," The Journal of
Psychohistory, 19, 2, 1991

There is hardly an imaginable form of genital assault that is not regularly performed on children.
Ibid.

Nothing can be more graphic of our hatred of children than an infant mortality rate of American babies in some of our largest cities that is close to that of a Third World country, or than the fact that we tolerate the regular use of poisonous drugs by millions of our teenagers. That we choose to buy aircraft carriers at the price of dead children may not be obvious, but it is true nonetheless.
LLOYD deMAUSE, "It's Time to Sacrifice... Our Children," *The Journal of Psychohistory,* 18, 2, 1990

When I can no longer bear to think of the victims of broken homes, I begin to think of the victims of intact ones.
PETER DE VRIES, *The Tunnel of Love,* 8, 1954

Every baby born into the world is a finer one than the last.
CHARLES DICKENS, *The Life and Adventures of Nicholas Nickleby,* 36, 1839

In the little world in which children have their existence, whosoever brings them up, there is nothing so finely perceived and so finely felt as injustice.
CHARLES DICKENS, *Great Expectations,* 9, 1861

Children have to be educated, but they have also to be left to educate themselves.
ERNEST DIMNET, *The Art of Thinking,* 2.5, 1928

The values inculcated by status-insecure parents are such that their children learn to put personal success and the acquisition of power above all else. They are taught to judge people for their usefulness rather than their likableness. Their friends, and even future marriage partners, are selected and used in the service of personal advancement; love and affection take second place to knowing the right people. They are taught to eschew weakness and passivity, to respect authority, and to despise those who have not made the socio-economic grade. Success is equated with social esteem and material advantage, rather than with more spiritual values.
NORMAN F. DIXON, *On the Psychology of Military Incompetence,* 22, 1976

How is it that little children are so intelligent and men so stupid? It must be education that does it.
ALEXANDER DUMAS (1802-1870), in L. Treich, *L'Esprit Francais,* 1947

So long as little children are allowed to suffer, there is no true love in this world.
ISADORA DUNCAN, "Memoirs," 1924, *This Quarter,* Autumn 1929

Come mothers and fathers
Throughout the land
And don't criticize
What you can't understand
Your sons and your daughters
Are beyond your command
Your old road is
Rapidly agin'.
Please get out of the new one
If you can't lend your hand
For the times they are a-changin'.
BOB DYLAN, "The Times They Are A-Changin" (song), 1963

Parents forgive their children least readily for the faults they themselves instilled in them.
> MARIE von EBNER-ESCHENBACH, *Aphorisms,* p. 31, 1880-1905, tr. David Scrase and Wolfgang Mieder, 1994

That was and still is the great disaster of my life – that lovely, lovely little boy. . . . There's no tragedy in life like the death of a child. Things never get back to the way they were.
> DWIGHT D. EISENHOWER (1890-1969), on the death of his first son Doud Dwight ("Icky") at age three, in "Ike," television documentary, PBS, 15 October 1986

I like my boy with his endless sweet soliloquies and iterations and his utter inability to conceive why I should not leave all my nonsense, business, and writing and come to tie up his toy horse, as if there was or could be any end to nature beyond his horse. And he is wiser than we when [he] threatens his whole threat "I will not love you."
> RALPH WALDO EMERSON, journal, 9 July 1839

It is so easy to give a naughty boy a slap, overpower him in an instant, and make him obey, that in this world of hurry and distraction, who can possibly spend time to wait for the slow return of his reason and the conquest of himself in the uncertainty too whether that will ever come.
> Ibid., 9 November 1839

My son, a perfect little boy of five years and three months, had ended his earthly life. You can never sympathize with me; you can never know how much of me such a young child can take away. A few weeks ago I accounted myself a very rich man, and now the poorest of all.
> RALPH WALDO EMERSON, soon after Waldo's death from scarlet fever, letter to Thomas Carlyle, 28 February 1842

Children measure their own life by the reaction, and if purring and humming [are] not noticed, they begin to squeal; if that is neglected, to screech; then, if you chide and console them, they find the experiment succeeds, and they begin again. The child will sit in your arms if you do nothing, contented; but if you read, it misses the reaction, and commences hostile operations.
RALPH WALDO EMERSON, journal, October? 1843

The cardinal virtue of a teacher [is] to protect the pupil from his own influence.
RALPH WALDO EMERSON, "Notebook Platoniana," p. 11, 1845-1848

We find a delight in the beauty and happiness of children that makes the heart too big for the body.
RALPH WALDO EMERSON, "Illusions," *The Conduct of Life,* 1860

A low self love in the parent desires that his child should repeat his character and fortune. . . . I suffer whenever I see that common sight of a parent or senior imposing his opinion and way of thinking and being on a young soul to which they are totally unfit. Cannot we let people be themselves, and enjoy life in their own way? You are trying to make another you. One's enough.
RALPH WALDO EMERSON (1803-1882), "Education," *Lectures and Biographical Sketches,* 1883

The secret of Education lies in respecting the pupil. It is not for you to choose what he shall know, what he shall do. It is chosen and foreordained, and he only holds the key to his own secret. . . . Respect the child. Wait and see the new product of Nature. Nature loves analogies, but not repetitions. Respect the child. Be not too much his parent. Trespass not on his solitude.
Ibid.

*Of course you will insist on modesty in the children, and respect to
their teachers, but if the boy stops you in your speech, cries out that
you are wrong and sets you right, hug him!*
Ibid.

The flowers talk when the wind blows over them.
WALDO EMERSON, at age 4, in Ralph Waldo Emerson, journal, 4
June 1840

*The report of the Central Commission relates that the manufacturers
began to employ children rarely of five years, often of six, very often of
seven, usually of eight to nine years; that the working day often lasted
fourteen to sixteen hours, exclusive of meals and intervals; that the
manufacturers permitted overlookers to flog and maltreat children,
and often took an active part in so doing themselves.*
FRIEDRICH ENGELS, *The Conditions of the Working Class in
England in 1844,* 1887

*[In cases of enuresis, i.e., bedwetting] I apply usually [in the region of
the boy's sexual organ] a tolerably strong current for one to two minutes; at the close, a wire electrode is introduced about two centimeters
into the urethra – in girls I apply "small" sponge electrode between
the labia close to the meatus urethrae – and the faradic current
passed for one to two minutes with such a strength that a distinct,
somewhat painful sensation is produced.*
WILHELM ERB, *Handbook of Electrotherapy,* 1881, in Thomas S.
Szasz, *The Myth of Psychotherapy,* 6.1, 1978

When I was a boy I was my father.
LAWRENCE FERLINGHETTI, "Mock Confessional," *Open Eye, Open
Heart,* 1973

How children survive being Brought Up amazes me.
MALCOLM S. FORBES, "Passing Parade," *The Sayings of Chairman
Malcolm: The Capitalist's Handbook,* 1978

How true Daddy's words were when he said: "All children must look after their own upbringing." Parents can only give good advice or put them on the right paths, but the final forming of a person's character lies in their own hands.
> ANNE FRANK, 15 July 1944, *Anne Frank: The Diary of a Young Girl,* tr. B. M. Mooyaart-Doubleday, 1952

Wise parents offer criticism only when asked, and then minimally.
> LEONARD ROY FRANK

Wise teachers create an environment that encourages students to teach themselves.
> Ibid.

Wise teachers impart their knowledge; inept ones impose theirs.
> Ibid.

What a difference it makes to come home to a child!
> MARGARET FULLER, letter to friends, 1849

At a good Table we may go to School.
> THOMAS FULLER, ed., *Gnomologia: Adages and Proverbs,* 823, 1732

Of some forty families I have been able to observe, I know hardly four in which the parents do not act in such a way that nothing would be more desirable for the child than to escape their influence.
> ANDRÉ GIDE, journal, 1921 (detached page), tr. Justin O'Brien, 1948

If children grew up according to early indications, we should have nothing but geniuses.
> GOETHE (1749-1832), in Norman Lockridge, ed., *World's Wit and Wisdom,* p. 352, 1936

Unlike grownups, children have little need to deceive themselves.
> GOETHE (1749-1832), in W. H. Auden and Louis Kronenberger, eds., *The Viking Book of Aphorisms,* p. 385, 1962

When an order is given to someone under hypnosis that he do something at a certain time after he is brought back to consciousness he will do his best to conform to the order however absurd it might be. If he is prevented *from fulfilling the order, he will have stirrings of acute guilt and anxiety. Most parents expect a great deal from their children when they grow up. . . . Suggestions made to children when very young have the same effect as a post-hypnotic suggestion – the child's whole life may be lived with an anxious feeling that he should be doing something other than what he is doing, that he should be a "better" person than he is, should be cleverer, more musical, a better athlete or whatever it might be.*
> FELIX GREENE, *The Enemy: What Every American Should Know About Imperialism,* 4.2, 1970

[The parents of prodigies] convey enthusiasm without conveying expectation. They reward their children more for trying than winning.
> EMILY GREENSPAN, Little Winners, 1983, in Jan Krakauer, "What Kind of Breakfast Are They Feeding These Young Champions?" *Washington Post National Weekly Edition,* 15 February 1988

Never do for a child what he is capable of doing for himself.
> ELIZABETH G. HAINSTOCK, *Teaching Montessori in the Home,* 1, 1968

I will hug him, so that not any storm can come to him.
> JULIAN HAWTHORNE, at 2 years and 8 months, speaking of his infant friend, in Nathaniel Hawthorne, 16 March 1849, *The American Notebooks,* ed. Claude M. Simpson, 1932

Nathaniel Hawthorne: Are you a good little boy?
Julian: Yes.
Nathaniel: [Why] are you good?
Julian: Because I love all people.
> Ibid., format adopted, 6 September 1849

Julian: Mamma, why is not dinner supper?
Mamma: Why is not a chair a table?
Julian: Because it's a teapot.
  Ibid., 4 October 1849

I said to Julian, "Let me take off your bib" – and he taking no notice, I
repeated it two or three times, each time louder than before. At last he
bellowed – "Let me take off your Head!"
  Ibid., 20 February 1850

[Towards the end of a long buggy trip in the country now under a full
moon] the little man behaved himself still like an old traveller; but
sometimes he looked round at me from the front seat (where he sat
between Herman Melville and Evert Duyckinck) and smiled at me
with a peculiar expression, and put back his hand to touch me. It was
a method of establishing a sympathy in what doubtless appeared to
him the wildest and unprecedentedest series of adventures that had
ever befallen mortal travellers.
  NATHANIEL HAWTHORNE, referring to his son Julian then 5 years
  old, 8 August 1851, *The American Notebooks,* ed. Claude M.
  Simpson, 1932

Virtue and a Trade are the best portion for Children.
  GEORGE HERBERT (1593-1633), ed., *Outlandish Proverbs,* 107, 1640

Better a snotty child than his nose wip'd off.
  Ibid., 828

Babies are such a nice way to start people.
  DON HEROLD (1889-1966), in Laurence J. Peter, *The Peter*
  Prescription, 12, 1972

He does not educate children but rejoices in their happiness.
  HERMANN HESSE (1877-1962), *Reflections,* 324, ed. Volker Michels,
  1974

I remember a lot of talk and a lot of laughter. I must have talked a great deal because Martha used to say again and again, "You remember you said this, you said that...." She remembered everything I said, and all my life I've had the feeling that what I think and what I say are worth remembering. She gave me that.
>   ERIC HOFFER, on Martha Bauer, the woman who raised him after his mother died, in Calvin Tompkins, "Profiles: The Creative Situation," *New Yorker,* 7 January 1967

The object of teaching a child is to enable him to get along without his teacher.
>   ELBERT HUBBARD, *A Thousand and One Epigrams,* p. 107, 1911

Be patient with the boys — you are dealing with soul-stuff.
>   ELBERT HUBBARD (1856-1915), *The Note Book of Elbert Hubbard,* ed., Elbert Hubbard II, p. 78, 1927

Where parents do too much for their children, the children will not do much for themselves.
>   Ibid., p. 193

I have noticed that youngsters given to the climbing habit usually do something when they grow up.
>   ELBERT HUBBARD (1856-1915), *The Philosophy of Elbert Hubbard,* ed., Elbert Hubbard II, p. 72, 1930

When I was a kid, my father told me every day, "You're the most wonderful boy in the world, and you can do anything you want to."
>   JAN HUTCHINS, radio talk-program host, KGO, San Francisco, 17 May 1988

No day can be so sacred but that the laugh of a little child will make it holier still.
>   ROBERT G. INGERSOLL, "Liberty of Man, Woman and Child," *The Lectures of Col. R. G. Ingersoll: Latest,* 1898

We are the world,
We are the children,
We are the ones
To make a better day.
MICHAEL JACKSON and LIONEL RICHIE, "We Are the World"
(song), 1985

It is while we are young that the habit of industry is formed. If not
then, it never is afterwards. The fortune of our lives, therefore,
depends on employing well the short period of youth.
THOMAS JEFFERSON, letter to his daughter Martha, 28 March 1787

Let the children come to me, do not hinder them; for to such belongs
the kingdom of God.
JESUS, *Mark* 10:14 (Revised Standard Version)

Accustom your children constantly to this; if a thing happened at one
window and they, when relating it, say that it happened at another,
do not let it pass, but instantly check them; you do not know where
deviation from truth will end.
SAMUEL JOHNSON, 31 March 1778, in James Boswell, *The Life of*
Samuel Johnson, 1791

There must always be a struggle between a father and son, while one
aims at power and the other at independence.
Ibid., 14 July 1763

Children have more need of models than of critics.
JOSEPH JOUBERT (1754-1824), *Pensées,* 1838, tr. Henry Attwell, 1877

Nothing exerts a stronger psychic effect upon the environment, and
especially upon children, than the [unlived] life [of] the parents.
CARL G. JUNG, "Paracelsus," 1929, *The Spirit in Man, Art, and*
Literature, tr. R. F. C. Hull, 1966

If there is anything that we wish to change in our children, we should first examine it and see whether it is not something that could better be changed in ourselves.
>CARL G. JUNG, title essay, 1934, *The Development of Personality,* tr. R. F. C. Hull, 1954

It is not that what is purveyed to [children] is always directly hurtful, intentionally or otherwise. Some of it even tries to be helpful. The evil lies rather in the forfeiture of what the child might otherwise be doing if he or she were not watching television.
>GEORGE F. KENNAN, *Around the Cragged Hill: A Personal and Political Philosophy,* 8, 1993

TWO THINGS I ALWAYS KNEW ABOUT YOU ONE THAT YOU ARE SMART TWO THAT YOU ARE A SWELL GUY LOVE DAD.
>JOSEPH P. KENNEDY, cable to his son John on hearing that he had won scholastic honors at Harvard University, 1940, in James MacGregor Burns, *John Kennedy: A Political Profile,* 3, 1959

Whenever I held my newborn baby in my arms, I used to think that what I said and did to him could have an influence not only on him but on all whom he met, not only for a day or a month or a year, but for all eternity – a very, very challenging and exciting thought for a mother.
>ROSE KENNEDY, in Gail Cameron, *Rose,* 5, 1971

God could not be everywhere, so He created mothers.
>LEOPOLD KOMPERT (1822-1886), in Joseph L. Baron, ed., *A Treasury of Jewish Quotations,* p. 319, 1956

One's first social identity is conferred on one. We learn to be whom we are told we are.
>R. D. LAING, *Self and Others,* 6, 1961

They fuck you up, your mum and dad.
  They may not mean to, but they do.
They fill you with the faults they had
  And add some extra, just for you.
But they were fucked up in their turn
  By fools in old-style hats and coats,
Who half the time were soppy-stern
  And half at one another's throats.
> PHILIP LARKIN, "This Be the Verse," 1971, *High Windows*, 1974

She's leaving home after living alone
For so many years. . . .
Something inside that was always denied
For so many years.
> JOHN LENNON and PAUL McCARTNEY, "She's Leaving Home"
> (song), 1967

To this hour I cannot really understand why little children are not just as constantly laughing as they are constantly crying.
> GEORG CHRISTOPH LICHTENBERG (1742-1799), *Aphorisms*, K.32,
> 1806, tr. R. J. Hollingdale, 1990

I can say this, that among my earliest recollections I remember how, when a mere child, I used to get irritated when anybody talked to me in a way I could not understand. . . . I can remember going to my little bedroom, after hearing the neighbors talk of an evening with my father, and spending no small part of the night walking up and down, and trying to make out what was the exact meaning of some of their, to me, dark sayings. I could not sleep, though I often tried to, when I got on such a hunt after an idea, until I had caught it; and when I

*thought I had got it, I was not satisfied until I had repeated it over
and over, until I had put it in language plain enough, as I thought, for
any boy I knew to comprehend.*
    ABRAHAM LINCOLN, remarks to the author, in Rev. J. P. Gulliver,
    New York Independent, 1 September 1864, repr. in F. B. Carpenter,
    Six Months at the White House with Abraham Lincoln, 77, 1866

*It is my pleasure that my children are free and happy, and unre-
strained by parental tyranny. Love is the chain whereby to bind a
child to its parents.*
    ABRAHAM LINCOLN (1809-1865), frequent remark to his wife Mary,
    in William H. Herndon (and Jesse W. Weik), Herndon's *Lincoln*, 17,
    1889, Premier Books edition, 1961

*Supported by the authority of all institutions, parenthood has come to
amount to little more than a campaign against individuality. Every
father and every mother trembles lest an offspring, in act or thought,
should be different from his fellows; and the smallest display of
uniqueness in a child becomes the signal for the application of drastic
measures aimed at stamping out that small fire of noncompliance by
which personal distinctness is expressed. In an atmosphere of anxiety,
in a climate of apprehension, the parental conspiracy against children is planned.*
    ROBERT LINDNER, *Prescription for Rebellion*, 3, 1952

*Only by being permitted to experience the consequences of his actions
will the child acquire a sense of responsibility; and within the limits
marked by the demands of his safety this must be done. From such
training we can expect many benefits to the person, one of which certainly will be the development of a natural rather than an imposed
control over [himself].*
    Ibid., 9

You must adjust. . . . *This is the legend imprinted in every school-book, the invisible message on every blackboard. Our schools have become vast factories for the manufacture of robots.*
ROBERT LINDNER, title essay (3), *Must You Conform?* 1956

You must do nothing before him, which you would not have him imitate.
JOHN LOCKE, *Some Thoughts Concerning Education,* 71, 1693

One great Reason why many Children abandon themselves wholly to silly sports and trifle away all their time insipidly is because they have found their **Curiosity** *baulk'd and their* **Enquiries** *neglected. But had they been treated with more Kindness and Respect and their* **Questions** *answered, as they should, to their Satisfaction, I doubt not but they would have taken more Pleasure in Learning and improving their Knowledge. . . than in returning over and over to the same Play and Playthings.*
Ibid., 118

There cannot be a greater Spur to the attaining [of] what you would have the Eldest learn. . . than to set him upon **teaching it** *[to]* **his younger Brothers** *and* **Sisters.**
Ibid., 119

[Learning] must never be imposed as a Task, nor made a Trouble to them. There may be Dice and Playthings with the Letters on them to teach Children the **Alphabet** *by playing; and twenty other Ways may be found, suitable to their particular Tempers, to make this kind of* **Learning a Sport** *to them.*
Ibid., 148

*If those about him will talk to him often about the Stories he has read
and hear him tell them, it will besides other Advantages, add
Encouragement and Delight to his **Reading**, when he finds there is
some Use and Pleasure in it.*
Ibid., 156

*Ye are better than all the ballads
   That ever were sung or said;
For ye are living poems,
   And all the rest are dead.*
HENRY WADSWORTH LONGFELLOW, last stanza, "Children," *Birds
of Passage,* 1858

*Children are God's apostles, day by day
Sent forth to preach of love, and hope, and peace.*
JAMES RUSSELL LOWELL, "On the Death of a Friend's Child," 1844

*And we remember the old stories,
   we remember how it began in the press of war.
Oh our ancestors in the press of war
   were seeking new and larger ways to kill.*

*And they opened the nucleus of the atom,
And with great effort and with great acumen
   and with great applications of their brains,
they made and exploded the first nucleus weapon,
   and the project, God forgive them,
they called Trinity
   in the desert of Alamo Gordo.*

*And the stories come down to us of a president called
   True Man
at a place called Pots Damn*

receiving a telegram:
"Baby safely delivered!"

And that baby was the poison fire.
JOANNA MACY, from the script of "The Standard Remembering of
Our Ancestors in the Times of Nuclear Peril" (often presented at her
workshops as part of an imagined visit to a future waste-storage
Guardian Site)

If a mother respects both herself and her child from his very first day
onward, she will never need to teach him respect for others.
ALICE MILLER, forward to *The Drama of the Gifted Child,* 1979, tr.
Ruth Ward, 1981

The child has a primary need to be regarded and respected as the per-
son he really is at any given time, and as the center – the central
actor – in his own activity.
Ibid., 1

We suppress the child's curiosity (for example, there are questions one
should not ask), and then when he lacks a natural interest in learn-
ing he is offered special coaching for his scholastic difficulties.
Ibid., 3

Patriarchy's chief institution is the family. It is both a mirror of and a
connection with the larger society; a patriarchal unit within a patri-
archal whole. Mediating between the individual and the social struc-
ture, the family affects control and conformity where political and
other authorities are insufficient. . . . Serving as an agent of the larger
society, the family not only encourages its own members to adjust
and conform, but acts as a unit in the government of the patriarchal
state which rules its citizens through its family heads.
KATE MILLET, *Sexual Politics,* 2.3, 1969

The greatest triumph of our educational method should always be this: to bring about the spontaneous progress of the child.
MARIA MONTESSORI, *The Montessori Method,* 15, tr. Anne E. George, 1912

There must be a suitable environment for the child's growth. Obstacles must be reduced to a minimum and the surroundings should provide the necessary means for the exercise of those activities which develop a child's energies. Since adults are also a part of a child's environment, they should adapt themselves to his needs.
MARIA MONTESSORI, *The Secret of Childhood,* 18, 1938, tr. M. Joseph Costelloe, 1972

The most striking [way in which children respond to external influences] and one that is almost like a magic wand for opening the gate to the normal expression of a child's natural gifts is activity concentrated on some task that requires movement of the hands guided by the intellect.
Ibid., 20

A child does not look for gain or assistance. A child must carry out his work by himself, and he must bring it to completion. No one can bear a child's burden and grow up in his stead. Nor is it possible for a child to speed up the rate of his development. One of the special characteristics of a growing being is that it must follow a kind of schedule that does not admit delays or accelerations.
Ibid., 27

[The child is] one guided by his inward teacher, who labors indefatigably in joy and happiness – following a precise timetable – at the work of constructing that greatest marvel of the Universe, the human being. We teachers can only help the work going on, as servants wait upon a master.
MARIA MONTESSORI, *The Absorbent Mind,* 1, 1949, tr. Claude A. Claremont, 1969

Whatever intelligent activity we chance to witness in a child – even if it seems absurd to us, or contrary to our wishes (provided, of course, that it does him no harm) – we must not interfere; for the child must always be able to finish the cycle of activity on which his heart is set.
Ibid., 15

Every defect of character is due to some wrong treatment sustained by the child during his early years.
Ibid., 17

No social problem is as universal as the oppression of the child.
MARIA MONTESSORI (1870-1952), *The Child in the Family*, 1, 1956, tr. Nancy Rockmore Cirillo, 1970

At particular epochs of their life, [children] reveal an intense and extraordinary interest in certain objects and exercises, which one might look for in vain at a later age. . . . Such attention is not the result of mere curiosity; it is more like a burning passion. A keen emotion first rises from the depths of the unconscious, and sets in motion a marvelous creative activity in contact with the outside world, thus building up consciousness.
MARIA MONTESSORI (1870-1952), on "sensitivity periods," in E. M. Standing, *Maria Montessori*, 7, 1957

It is easy to substitute our will for that of the child by means of suggestion or coercion; but when we have done this we have robbed him of his greatest right, the right to construct his own personality.
Ibid., 14

Those parents are wisest who train their sons and daughters in the utmost liberty both of thought and speech; who do not instill dogmas into them, but inculcate upon them the sovereign importance of correct ways of forming opinions.
JOHN MORLEY, *On Compromise*, 4, 1877

One would be in less danger
From the wiles of the stranger
If one's own kin and kith
Were more fun to be with.
OGDEN NASH, "Family Court," *Many Long Years Ago,* 1945

Children are inclined to learn from television [because]... it is never
too busy to talk to them, and it never has to brush them aside while it
does household chores. Unlike their preoccupied parents, television
seems to want their attention at any time, and goes to considerable
lengths to attract it.
NATIONAL COMMISSION ON THE CAUSES AND PREVENTION OF
VIOLENCE, in "Excerpts from National Panel's Statement on
Violence in TV Entertainment," *New York Times,* 25 September 1969

Children begin with the intuition that the noises produced by people
around them can be related either to what they already know or to
what they can discover about the world. Children do not extract
meaning from what they hear others saying; they try, instead, to
relate what has been said to what is going on.
JUDITH M. NEWMAN, ed., *Whole Language: Theory in Use,* 4, 1985

Children seem to learn to talk by inventing their own words and
rules: by experimenting with language. Children make statements in
their own language for meanings which are perfectly obvious to
adults and then wait for adults to put the statements into adult lan-
guage so they can make a comparison. . . . If the adult says nothing or
simply continues the conversation, the child assumes his or her utter-
ance is correct. When adults "correct" – that is, expand in adult lan-
guage what children have said – they are providing feedback. The
adult and the child are actually speaking different languages, but
because they understand the situation, the child can compare their
different ways of saying the same thing. . . . The process is one of suc-
cessive approximations toward adult forms of expression.
Ibid.

The child is innocence and forgetfulness, a new beginning, a sport, a self-propelling wheel, a first motion, a sacred Yes.
FRIEDRICH NIETZSCHE, "Of the Three Metamorphoses," *Thus Spoke Zarathustra*, 1892, tr. R. J. Hollingdale, 1961

All babies are born singing God's name. . . .
All babies are born out of great pain
over and over
All born into great pain
All babies are crying
for no one remembers God's name.
SINEAD O'CONNOR, "All Babies" (song), 1994

The perjurer's mother told white lies.
AUSTIN O'MALLEY (1858-1932), in Norman Lockridge, ed., *World's Wit and Wisdom*, p. 479, 1936

There are families in which the father will say to his child, "You'll get a thick ear if you do that again," while the mother, her eyes brimming over with tears, will take the child in her arms and murmur lovingly, "Now, darling, is it kind to Mummy to do that?" And who would maintain that the second method is less tyrannous than the first?
GEORGE ORWELL, "Lear, Tolstoy and the Fool," March 1947, The Collected Essays, Journalism and Letters of George Orwell, vol. 4, ed. Sonia Orwell and Ian Angus, 1968

A show can "appeal" to a child. . . without necessarily offering the child amusement or pleasure. It appeals if it helps him express his inner tensions and fantasies in a manageable way. It appeals if it gets him a little scared or mad or befuddled and then offers him a way to get rid of his fear, anger, or befuddlement.
VANCE PACKARD, summarizing a finding from a television motivational research study entitled "Now, for the Kiddies...," *The Hidden Persuaders*, 15, 1957

What God is to the world, parents are to their children.
PHILO (20 B.C.-40 A.D.), *Honor Due to Parents*

Do not use compulsion, but let early education be rather a sort of amusement; you will then be better able to find out the natural bent.
PLATO (427?-347 B.C.), *The Republic,* 7.536-537, tr. Benjamin Jowett, 1894

Children's liberation is the next item on our civil rights shopping list.
LETTY COTTIN POGREBIN, "Down with Sexist Upbringing," in Francine Klagsbrun, ed., *The First Ms. Reader,* 1972

'Tis Education forms the common mind,
Just as the Twig is bent, the Tree's inclin'd.
ALEXANDER POPE, *Moral Essays,* 1.101, 1731-1735

One cardinal principle might be named, that of maximum reasonable autonomy: the child (or for that matter anyone) should be free to act unless harmful consequences can be clearly shown.
JOHN RADFORD, *Child Prodigies and Exceptional Early Achievers,* 11, 1990

Few have been taught to any purpose who have not been their own teachers. We prefer those instructions which we have given ourselves, from our affection [for] the instructor.
SIR JOSHUA REYNOLDS, "Discourse Two," 11 December 1769, *Discourses on Art,* 1769-1790

At the end of the visit, Diana reviews the events and the learning with the children. She asks the children their favorite event. "The alone walk," they all clamor. Walking all alone along the trail. Each one being brave, courageous. Discovering that they can find their own way.
LOIS ROBIN, referring to a schoolchildren's outing with Diana Almendariz, a Native American cultural interpreter, a descendent of the Nisenan-Maidu tribe, "A Day with Diana," *News from Native California,* Fall 1991

School is an invaluable adjunct to the home, but it is a wretched substitute for it.
THEODORE ROOSEVELT (1858-1919), in Hermann Hagedorn and
Sidney Wallach, "Signposts for Americans: Character and
Conduct," *A Theodore Roosevelt Round-Up,* 1958

Why do grown-ups always say, "Don't hit," and then they go and start a big war?
BENJAMIN ROTTMAN, letter to *Los Angeles Times,* quoted in "The
War Some Wanted," *Progressive,* March 1991

It is not [a child's] hearing of the word, but its accompanying intonation that is understood.
ROUSSEAU, *Emile; or, Treatise on Education,* 1, 1762, tr. Barbara
Foxley, 1911

Since everything that comes into the human mind enters through the gates of sense, man's first reason is a reason of sense-experience. It is this that serves as a foundation for the reason of the intelligence; our first teachers in natural philosophy are our feet, hands, and eyes. To substitute books for them does not teach us to reason, it teaches us to use the reason of others rather than our own; it teaches us to believe much and know little.
Ibid., 2

Teach your scholar to observe the phenomena of nature; you will soon rouse his curiosity, but if you would have it grow, do not be in too great a hurry to satisfy this curiosity. Put the problems before him and let him solve them himself. Let him know nothing because you have told him, but because he has learned it for himself. Let him not be taught science, let him discover it. If ever you substitute authority for reason, he will cease to reason; he will be a mere plaything of other people's thoughts.
Ibid., 3

As soon as he begins to reason let there be no comparison with other children, no rivalry, no competition, not even in running races. I would far rather he did not learn anything than have him learn it through jealousy or self-conceit. Year by year I shall just note the progress he had made, I shall compare the results with those of the [previous] year, I shall say, "You have grown so much; that is the ditch you jumped, the weight you carried. . . etc.; let us see what you can do now."
Ibid.

The teacher's art consists in this: To turn the child's attention from trivial details and to guide his thoughts continually towards relations of importance which he will one day need to know, that he may judge rightly of good and evil in society.
Ibid.

The revolution declares war on Original Sin, the dictatorship of parents over their kids.
JERRY RUBIN, *Do It! Scenarios of the Revolution,* 20, 1970

If a child is reading aloud to you and comes to a word she doesn't understand, don't immediately ask her to sound it out. Instead, say, "What makes sense here?" Then the child has to think about how that word fits in with what she's been reading.
MASHA KABAKOW RUDMAN (educator [University of Massachusetts]), in Lawrence Kutner, "Improved Reading Begins at Home, Where a Child Can See How Reading Fits in with Other Activities," *New York Times,* 17 December 1992

Give a little love to a child, and you get a great deal back. It loves everything near it, when it is a right kind of child – would hurt nothing, would give the best it has away. . . and delights in helping people; you cannot please it so much as by giving it a chance of being useful, in ever so little a way.
JOHN RUSKIN, "Work," *The Crown of Wild Olive,* 1866

Almost all education has a political motive: it aims at strengthening some group, national or religious or even social, in the competition with other groups. It is this motive, in the main, which determines the subjects taught, the knowledge offered and the knowledge withheld, and also decides what mental habits the pupils are expected to acquire. Hardly anything is done to foster the inward growth of mind and spirit; in fact, those who have had most education are very often atrophied in their mental and spiritual life.
BERTRAND RUSSELL, *Principles of Social Reconstruction*, 5, 1916

If the object [of education] were to make pupils think, rather than to make them accept certain conclusions, education would be conducted quite differently; there would be less. . . instruction and more discussion.
Ibid.

Education should not aim at a passive awareness of dead facts, but at an activity directed towards the world that our efforts are to create.
Ibid.
Children learn at their own pace, and it is a mistake to try to force them. The great incentive to effort, all through life, is experience of success after initial difficulties. The difficulties must not be so great as to cause discouragement, or so small as not to stimulate effort. From birth to death, this is a fundamental principle. It is by what we do ourselves that we learn.
BERTRAND RUSSELL, *Education and the Good Life*, 3, 1926

Our system of education turns young people out of the schools able to read, but for the most part unable to weigh evidence or to form an independent opinion.
BERTRAND RUSSELL, *Sceptical Essays*, 12, 1928

A baby is God's opinion that life should go on.
CARL SANDBURG, *Remembrance Rock*, 2, 1948

The human intellect is said to be so constituted that general ideas arise by abstraction from particular observations, and therefore come after them in point of time. . . .

Contrarily, the artificial method is to hear what other people say, to learn and to read, and so to get your head crammed full of general ideas before you have any sort of extended acquaintance with the world as it is, and as you may see it for yourself.
ARTHUR SCHOPENHAUER, "Studies in Pessimism: On Education,"
Essays of Arthur Schopenhauer, tr. T. Bailey Saunders, 1851
[In the next paragraph Schopenhauer commented that to acquire "general ideas" first and then make "particular observations" is like "putting the cart before the horse."]

Childhood and youth form the time for collecting materials, for getting a special and thorough knowledge of individual and particular things. In those years it is too early to form views on a large scale; and ultimate explanations must be put off to a later date. The faculty of judgment, which cannot come into play without mature experience, should be left to itself; and care should be taken not to anticipate its action by inculcating prejudice, which will paralyze it forever.
Ibid.

There is no absurdity so palpable but that it may be firmly planted in the human head if you only begin to inculcate it before the age of five, by constantly repeating it with an air of great solemnity.
ARTHUR SCHOPENHAUER, "Studies in Pessimism: Further Psychological Observations," *Essays of Arthur Schopenhauer,* tr. T. Bailey Saunders, 1851

You must teach your children that the ground beneath their feet is the ashes of our grandfathers. So that they will respect the land, tell your children that the earth is rich with the lives of our kin. Teach your children what we have taught our children, that the earth is our mother. Whatever befalls the earth befalls the sons of the earth. If men spit upon the ground, they spit upon themselves.

This we know. The earth does not belong to man; man belongs to the earth. This we know. All things are connected like the blood which unites one family. All things are connected.

Whatever befalls the earth befalls the sons of the earth. Man does not weave the web of life, he is merely a strand in it. Whatever he does to the web, he does to himself
> CHIEF SEATTLE, speech delivered before a tribal assembly in Duwamish in the Pacific northwest, 1854 (from notes taken by Dr. Henry Smith)

They taught their children nothing that they had to learn sitting.
> SENECA the YOUNGER (4? B.C.-65 A.D.), in Montaigne, "Against Do-Nothingness," *Essays*, 1588, tr. Donald M. Frame, 1958

Desdemona: Those that do teach young babes
Do it with gentle means and easy tasks.
> SHAKESPEARE, *Othello*, 4.2.111, 1604

The Carnegie [Corporation] report [Starting Points: Meeting the Needs of Our Youngest Children, 1994] compares the brain of a newborn child to a tangled and unconnected mass of electronic circuitry. As a child begins to recognize things around him — "to make connections" — the circuity becomes organized. . . .
　Parents play a critical role in helping a baby organize this neural circuitry. When they talk or sing to a child or play with him, they are doing more than amusing the child; they are providing stimulation that is essential to the maturation of the child's brain. If they or some-one else does not provide this stimulation, his development will be permanently impaired.
> ALBERT SHANKER, "The High Price of Neglect" (advertisement), *New York Times*, 27 November 1994

This is my father, Mrs. Baines. Try what you can do with him. He won't listen to me because he remembers what a fool I was when I was a baby.
GEORGE BERNARD SHAW, *Major Barbara*, 2, 1905

Parents set themselves to bend the will of their children to their own – to break their stubborn spirit, as they call it – with the ruthlessness of Grand Inquisitors. Cunning, unscrupulous children learn all the arts of the sneak in circumventing tyranny: children of better character are cruelly distressed and more or less lamed for life by it.
GEORGE BERNARD SHAW, "The Demagogue's Opportunity," *Parents and Children*, 1914

If for only half an hour a day, a child should do something serviceable to the community.
Ibid., "The Horror of the Perpetual Holiday"

Every child has a right to its own bent. . . . It has a right to find its own way and go its own way, whether that way seems wise or foolish to others, exactly as an adult has. It has a right to privacy as to its own doings and its own affairs as much as if it were its own father.
Ibid., "The Manufacture of Monsters"

"Wanted: A Child's Magna Charta."
Ibid., section heading

The imprisonment, the beating, the taming and laming, the breaking of young spirits, the arrest of development, the atrophy of all inhibitive power except the power of fear, are real: the education is a sham. Those who have been taught most know least.
Ibid., "Why We Loathe Learning and Love Sport"

My schooling not only failed to teach me what it professed to be teaching, but prevented me from being educated to an extent which infuriates me when I think of all I might have learnt at home by myself.
GEORGE BERNARD SHAW, *Everybody's Political What's What?* 22, 1944

Freeman and Watts described the four-year-old [they lobotomized in 1943] as "absolutely incorrigible, destructive, assaultive," with "his face a mass of bruises" from self-inflicted injuries. "Unfortunately the possibility in this case will remain unknown," they wrote, "because after return home, and when things were going well, he contracted meningitis and died three weeks after the operation."
DAVID SHUTTS, *Lobotomy: Resort to the Knife,* 6, 1982

Let us put our minds together and see what we will make for our children.
CHIEF SITTING BULL, in Ronald Miller and the Editors of *New Age Journal,* eds., *As Above, So Below,* 1992

Don't laugh at a youth for his affectations; he is only trying on one face after another to find his own.
LOGAN PEARSALL SMITH, *Afterthoughts,* 2, 1931

To me, education is a leading out of what is already there in the pupil's soul. To Miss Mackay, it is a putting in of something that is not there, and that is not what I call education, I call it intrusion.
MURIEL SPARK, *The Prime of Miss Jean Brodie,* 2, 1961

At each age the intellectual action which a child likes is a healthful one for it. . . . The rise of one appetite for any kind of knowledge implies that the unfolding mind has become fit to assimilate it, and needs it for the purposes of growth. . . . On the other hand, the disgust

felt towards any kind of knowledge is a sign either that it is prema-turely presented, or that it is presented in an undigestible form.
    HERBERT SPENCER, *Education: Intellectual, Moral, and Physical,* 2, 1860

Teaching by principles – that is, the leaving of generalizations until there are particulars to base them on.
    Ibid.

*Children should be led to make their own investigations and to draw their own inferences. They should be **told** as little as possible and induced to **discover** as much as possible. Humanity has progressed solely by self-instruction. . . . If the subjects be put before him in right order and right form, any pupil of ordinary capacity will surmount his successive difficulties with but little assistance.*
    Ibid.

The defects of the children mirror the defects of their parents.
    Ibid., 3

*The aim of your discipline should be to produce a **self-governing** being, not to produce a being to be **governed by others.***
    Ibid.

My own course [of study] – not intentionally pursued, but sponta-neously pursued – may be characterized as little reading and much thinking, and thinking about facts learned at first hand.
    HERBERT SPENCER, letter to Leslie Stephen, 2 July 1899, 2 July 1899, in David Duncan, *Life and Letters of Herbert Spencer,* 2.23, 1908

A constant question with my father was, "Can you tell the cause of this?" So there was established a habit of seeking for causes, and a tacit belief in the universality of causation.
    HERBERT SPENCER (1820-1903), Autobiography, 1904

Perhaps a child who is fussed over gets a feeling of destiny, he thinks he is in the world for something important and it gives him drive and confidence.
BENJAMIN SPOCK, in *New York Daily News,*
11 May 1958

The adult works to perfect his environment, whereas the child works to perfect himself, using the environment as the means. . . . The child is a being in a constant state of transformation.
E. M. STANDING, *Maria Montessori: Her Life and Work,* 8, 1957

Concentration is the key that opens up to the child the latent treasures within him.
Ibid., 10

If you imitate a baby, that only shows you know what he did, not how he felt. To let him know you sense how he feels, you have to play back his inner feelings in another way. Then the baby knows he is understood.
DAVID STERN, psychiatrist, in Daniel Goleman, "Child Development Theory Stresses Small Moments," *New York Times,* 21 October 1986
[Goleman comments, "The main message is in the mother's more or less matching the baby's level of excitement," and later paraphrases Stern, "(the mother's imitative acts) give an infant the deeply reassuring sense of being emotionally connected to someone."]

Threats of any kind, from any source, stimulate an intense need for attachment on the part of the infant because the prime function of attachment is protection from the threat of danger. But if the source of the threat is the very person to whom the infant must turn for protection, the infant is faced with a conflict which cannot be resolved. Placed in such a situation, the infant exhibits vacillation between approach, avoidance, and angry behavior.
ANTHONY STORR, *Solitude: A Return to the Self,* 7, 1988

It is the securely attached child who is most able to leave the mother's side in order to explore the environment and investigate the objects which it contains. Thus, the earliest manifestation of "interests" cannot be regarded as a substitute for affectional ties, but rather as bearing witness to their adequacy.
Ibid., 10

[Growing up] is especially difficult to achieve for a child whose parents do not take him seriously; that is, who do not expect proper behavior from him, do not discipline him, and finally, do not respect him enough to tell him the truth.
THOMAS S. SZASZ, "Tragic Failures," *National Review,* 26 May 1972

Childhood is a prison sentence of twenty-one years.
THOMAS S. SZASZ, opening words, "Childhood," *The Second Sin,* 1973

Every child comes with the message that God is not yet discouraged of man.
RABINDRANATH TAGORE, *Stray Birds,* 77, 1914

*Remember the feeling as a child
when you woke up and morning smiled,
it's time you felt like that again.*
TAJ MAHAL, "Giant Step" (song)

*Happy he
With such a mother! faith in womankind
Beats with his blood, and truth in all things high
Comes easy to him.*
ALFRED, LORD TENNYSON, *The Princess; A Medley,* 7.308, 1847

The wildest colts make the best horses.
THEMISTOCLES (524?-460? B.C.), in Plutarch (46?-119? A.D.), "Themistocles," *Plutarch's Lives,* Dryden edition, 1693

Every child begins the world again.
   HENRY DAVID THOREAU, "Economy," *Walden; or Life in the Woods,* 1854

"What did we do wrong?" The hard answer is that failed parents tend to be failed people who use children for their own emotional hang-ups.
   TIME, "On Being an American Parent" (essay), 15 December 1967

Growing up is a dialectical process that requires things that one can push against in order to become stronger. It takes limited war against worthy opponents; a child matures by testing himself against limits set by loving adults.
   Ibid.

Neglect and ill-usage of children died hard. The streets of the slums were still the only playground for the majority of city children, few of whom had schools to go to until 1870, and none of whom had Play Centers till the turn of the Century. The Society for the Prevention of Cruelty to Children was not founded till 1844; since that year it has dealt effectively with more than five million cases.
   G. M. TREVELYAN, *English Social History: A Survey of Six Centuries, Chaucer to Queen Victoria,* 17, 1942

Always obey your parents — when they are present.
   MARK TWAIN, "Advice to Youth," speech, 1882

When I was a boy of 14, my father was so ignorant I could hardly stand to have the old man around. But when I got to be 21, I was astonished at how much the old man had learned in seven years.
   MARK TWAIN (1835-1910), in "Bringing Up Father" (p. 22), *Reader's Digest,* September 1937.
[This well-known observation, often attributed to Twain, has not been found in his writings.]

Iqbal Masih was an indentured servant in a carpet factory at age 4. He escaped six years later to become a crusader against child labor, closing down dozens of carpet factories in his native Pakistan and winning international acclaim for his work. Last week the 12-year-old, who wanted to be "the Abraham Lincoln of his people," was shot dead in his village. A local man was arrested for the crime, which some suspect was the work of the carpet industry.
　　U.S. NEWS & WORLD REPORT, "Outlook," 1 May 1995

The only avenue towards wisdom is by freedom in the presence of knowledge. But the only avenue towards knowledge is by discipline in the acquirement of ordered fact. Freedom and discipline are the two essentials of education. . . .

　The pupil's mind is a growing organism. On the one hand, it is not a box to be ruthlessly packed with alien ideas: and, on the other hand, the ordered acquirement of knowledge is the natural food for a developing intelligence. . . . The two principles, freedom and discipline, are not antagonists, but should be so adjusted in the child's life that they correspond to a natural sway, to and fro, of the developing personality.
　　ALFRED NORTH WHITEHEAD, *The Aims of Education and Other Essays,* 3 (chapter title: "The Rhythmic Claims of Freedom and Discipline"), 1929

There is no comprehension apart from romance. . . . Without the adventure of romance, at the best you get inert knowledge without initiative, and at the worst you get contempt of ideas – without ideas.
　　Ibid.

Children begin by loving their parents; as they grow older they judge them; sometimes they forgive them.
　　OSCAR WILDE, *The Picture of Dorian Gray,* 5, 1891

Schoolmasters and parents exist to be grown out of.
　　JOHN WOLFENDEN, in *Sunday Times* (London), 13 June 1958

The Child is father of the Man.
　　WILLIAM WORDSWORTH, "My Heart Leaps Up When I Behold," l.
　　7, 1807

Heaven lies about us in our infancy!
　　WILLIAM WORDSWORTH, "Ode. Intimations of Immortality from
　　Recollections of Early Childhood," 5, 1807

*The first gold star a child gets in school for the mere performance of a
needful task is its first lesson in graft.*
　　PHILIP WYLIE, *Generation of Vipers,* 7, 1942

Half close your eyelids, loosen your hair,
And dream about the great and their pride;
They have spoken against you everywhere,
But weigh this song with the great and their pride;
I made it out of a mouthful of air,
Their children's children shall say they have lied.
　　W. B. YEATS, complete poem, "He Thinks of Those Who Have
　　Spoken Evil of His Beloved," *The Wind Among the Reeds,* 1899

Anonymous: What do you want to be?
*Anonymous third-grader (in writing): I would like to be myself. I
tried to be other things, but I always failed.*
　　ANONYMOUS (AMERICAN), format adapted, in R. Buckminster
　　Fuller, *I Seem To Be a Verb,* p. 177, 1970

*There is a greater advance from the infant to the speaking child than
there is from the schoolboy to a Newton.*
　　ANONYMOUS (GERMAN), in E. M. Standing, *Maria Montessori,* 21,
　　1957

I make honorable things pleasant to children.
　　ANONYMOUS (GREEK), Spartan teacher when asked about his
　　method, in Plutarch (46?-119? A.D.), "Can Virtue Be Taught?" (1),
　　Moralia, vol. 6, tr. W. C. Helmbold, 1939

We do not inherit the earth from our ancestors; we borrow it from our children.
ANONYMOUS (NATIVE AMERICAN)

It takes a village to raise a child.
SAYING (AFRICAN)
[Compare, "It Takes a City to Raise a Child," Adair Lara, column headline, San Francisco Chronicle, 16 March 1995

Spare the rod and spoil the child.
SAYING (ENGLISH)
[Contrast, "Those who love their children spare the rod." Saying (Greek)]

An apple doesn't usually fall far from the tree.
SAYING (GERMAN)
[Contrast, "Many a fair flower springs out of a dunghill." Saying (New England) in Wolfgang Mieder, ed., "Chance and Fate," Yankee Wisdom: New England Proverbs, 1989]

What impact will this have on the seventh generation from today?
SAYING (NATIVE AMERICAN), Consideration during decision-making process.

Father knows best.
SAYING
[Contrast, "Mother Knows Best" (story title), Edna Ferber, 1927]

55 Hours or Nothing!
SLOGAN (AMERICAN), on signs carried by striking children at Philadelphia textile mills, 1903, in Stephen Donadio et al., eds., *The New York Library Book of Twentieth-Century American Quotations,* p. 413, 1992

References

Ayres, A. J. (1979) *Sensory Integration and the Child*. LA: Western Psychological Series.

Bradshaw, J. (1988) *Healing the Shame That Binds You*. Health Communications, Inc.

Breggin, P. (1991) *Toxic Psychiatry: Why Therapy, Empathy and Love Must Replace the Drugs, Electroshock and Biochemical Theories of the New Psychiatry*. St. Martin's Press.

Chapters 12 and 13 of this devastating critique speak right to the heart of abandoning responsibility for our children by labeling them with psychiatric "disorders" like ADHD and giving them drugs.

Breggin, P. & G. Breggin, (1994) *The War Against Children: How the Drugs, Programs, and Theories of the Psychiatric Establishment are Threatening America's Children with a Medical "Cure" for Violence*. St. Martin's Press.

Chapter 4 of this powerful expose is called "Born to be Disruptive." Highly recommended.

Cameron, J. with Bryan, M. (1992) *The Artist's Way: A Spiritual Path to Higher Creativity*. G. P. Putnam & Sons.

Colt, G.H. (1991) *The Enigma of Suicide*. Simon & Schuster.

Crook, W. (1991) *Help for the Hyperactive* Children. Professional Books.

An MD provides some good, clear guidance in dealing with nutritional and environmental factors in attention and behavior.

Dufty, W. (1975) *Sugar Blues*. Warren Books.

> Still the classic on the bad news of sugar consumption.

Elkind, D. (1988) *The Hurried Child: Growing up too Fast too Soon*. Addison-Wesley.

Frank, L. R. (1995) *Influencing Minds: A Reader in Quotations*. Feral House.

Glendinning, C. (1994) *My Name is Chellis and I Am In Recovery from Western Civilization*. Shambala.

Halpern, S. (1985) *Sound Health: The Music and Sounds That Make Us Whole*. Harper & Row.

Healy, J. (1990) *Endangered Minds: Why Our Children Don't Think*. Simon and Schuster.

> An impressive, carefully argued book about how electronic media, fast-paced life styles, environmental hazards and current educational practices affect our children's thinking. Really drives the point home about overstimulation.

Kushi, M. & Kushi, A., Esko, W. & Esko E. (1994) *Raising Healthy Kids*. Avery Press.

Macrobiotic viewpoint on food and children's health and behavior.

Levine, S. & Levine, O, (1995) *Embracing the Beloved: Relationship As a Path of Awakening*. Doubleday.

Liberman, J. (1991) *Light, Medicine of the Future*. Bear & Co., Inc.

> On the importance of sunlight and full-spectrum lighting.

Liedloff, J. (1985) *The Continuum Concept*. Addison-Wesley.

> I love this book for it's poignant reminder of how we've lost our way from the natural continuum of life in which we hold babies continuously "in-arms."

Lusseyran, J. (1963) *And There Was Light*. Parabola.

Mander, J. (1977) *Four Arguments for the Elimination of Television*. William Morrow/Quill.

Mander, J. (1991) *In The Absence of the Sacred: The Failure of Technology and the Survival of the Indian Nations*. Sierra Club Books.

> Chapters 5 and 6 confirm Mander's great work on television. His explanation of TV's "Acceleration of the Nervous System" is crucial to the problem of children's attention. I am also grateful for his great reminder of the importance of "downtime." (Pp. 83-84)

McGuinness, D. (1985) *When Children Don't Learn: Understanding the Biology and Psychology of Learning Disorders*. Basic Books.

> This wonderful book clearly shows the fallacies of a "hyperactive syndrome." A thorough research review shows that "Essentially nothing has been found," and that "stimulant drugs have failed in all cases to effect any improvement in academic ability."

McGuinness, D. (1989) *Attention Deficit Disorder: The Emperor's Clothes, Animal "Pharm," and Other Fiction. In The Limits of Biological Treatments for Psychological Distress*, S. Fisher & R.P. Greenberg (Eds.), Laurence Erlbaum Associates.

Mendelsohn, R. (1994) *How to Raise a Healthy Child in Spite of Your Doctor*. Contemporary Books.

Miller, A. (1990) *Banished Knowledge*. Doubleday.

Mindell, A. (1993) *The Shaman's Body*. Harper-Collins.

Oski, F. And Bell, J.D. (1977) *Don't Drink Your Milk*. Wyden Books.

Rapp, D.J., (1991) *Is This Your Child?* William Morrow.

> This book is on the use of diet and allergy extract

therapy. You can also call the Practical Allergy Research Foundation (PARF) in Buffalo, NY at (716) 875-0398 to locate an environmental medicine specialist in your area who can test for allergies.

Roszak, T. (1992) *The Voice of the Earth*. Simon & Schuster.

Sahley, B.J. (1994) *Control Hyperactivity. Pain and Stress* Center Publications.

To order her book or to get information about the "Calm Kids" formula, you can call the Pain, Stress and Therapy Center in San Antonio, TX (Telephone (800) 669-CALM or 210-614-PAIN).

Solter, A. (1989) *Helping Young Children Flourish*. Shining Star Press.

This is a fantastic book on how to think about and counsel young children. Most highly recommended.

Resources

CHILDREN FIRST!

Center for the Study of Psychiatry, 4628 Chestnut Street, Bethesda, MD 20814.

Children First! is the only national program that focuses on the dangers of BioPsychiatric interventions into the lives of children while supporting more caring alternatives. It needs your support to enlarge its national educational campaign against the wholesale diagnosing and drugging of America's children.

Children First! is a newly developed activity of the Center for the Study of Psychiatry. The center itself was founded in 1971 and is a non-profit, tax-exempt research and educational institute devoted to reform in mental health. The Center's Board of Directors and Advisory Council include more than 100 leading psychiatrists and other mental health professionals, attorneys, patient advocates, psychiatric survivors, and members of Congress.

Peter R. Breggin, M.D., is the Center director and Ginger Ross Breggin is the director of research and education. John George, Ed.D., and Michael Valentine, Ph.D., are co-directors of Children First! and can be reached through the Center.

Members receive a newsletter and the satisfaction of supporting these reform efforts on behalf of America's children. The annual membership fee for Children First! is $25.

Citizens Commission on Human Rights (CCHR)

International Office, 6362 Hollywood Blvd., Suite B, Los Angeles, CA 90028

Founded in 1969, Citizens Commission on Human Rights is a private, non-profit organization whose sole purpose is to investigate and expose psychiatric violations of human rights. To obtain a free information packet on Ritalin, call 1-800-869-2247.

Additional Resources
Associations and Agencies Helping Parents, Families, and/or Young Children

Family Resource Coalition
(Information, listings of support groups, & a newsletter)
230 N. Michigan Ave., Suite 1625
Chicago, IL 60601

Coalition for Children and Youth
(An information center)
815 15th St., NW
Washington, DC 02192

National Committee for Prevention of Child Abuse
332 S. Michigan Ave., Suite 950
Chicago IL 60604

International Society for Prevention of Child Abuse and Neglect
1205 Oneida St.
Denver, CO 80220

Parents Anonymous
(Support for parents concerned about abusing their children)
6733 S. Sepulveda, Suite 270
Los Angeles, CA 90045

Parents United
(Assistance to families affected by child sexual abuse)
P.O. Box 952
San Jose, CA 95108

Fatherhood Project
c/o Bank Street College of Education
610 W. 112th St.
New York. NY 10025

Mothers at Home
P.O. Box 2208
Merrifield, VA 22116

Parents Without Partners
8807 Colesville Rd.
Silver Spring, MD 20910

Parents Sharing Custody
435 N. Bedford Dr., Suite 310
Beverly Hills, CA 90210

Home School Legal Defense Association
P.O. Box 950
Great Falls, VA 22066

Growing Without Schooling
Holt Associates
(Publishes a newsletter)
2269 Massachusetts Ave.
Cambridge, MA 02140

National Coalition on Television Violence
P.O. Box 2157
Champaign, IL 61820

National Information Center for Handicapped Children and Youth
P.O. Box 1492
Washington, DC 20013

Re-Evaluation Counseling (RC)
P.O. Box 2081, Main Office Station
Seattle, WA 98111

About the Author

John Breeding, Ph.D. is a psychologist with a well-established private counseling practice in Austin, Texas. A significant part of his work involves counseling with parents and children. He also lectures and leads workshops for parents and educators on handling the challenge of a child who is labeled a "problem."

Dr. Breeding has published several newspaper and magazine articles on parents and children, including a 32-page booklet on the topic of this book. He has also done several related radio shows, and produced and distributed an audiotape on this topic. He is a clear, strong advocate for parents and young people.

Dr. Breeding is also a father. He has a 9 year-old son, Eric, and a 5 year-old daughter, Vanessa. He draws liberally from personal experience in writing this book.

The Wildest Colts Make the Best Horses is a thoughtful, forceful, and informative response to a major current societal phenomenon. An estimated two million school-age children are on Ritalin today; countless more are being confronted with diagnoses of attention deficit or other behavioral disorders. In this book, Dr. Breeding presents a powerful challenge to mainstream thought about this phenomenon. Parents and other caregivers are offered a well thought out alternative perspective, and clear specific guidance toward more helpful responses to the challenges of parents and children in today's world.

Wildest Colts Parenting Work
Products, Services and Workshops

Resources for parents in handling the challenge
of a child who is labeled a "problem"

offered by

John Breeding, Ph. D.

- Consultation with parents, teachers
  and other caregivers
- Education
- Training
- Workshops

To inquire about the above services,
please call John Breeding in Austin, Texas at
(512) 326-8326.

To Order Additional Copies of This Book

	Unit Price	Number Ordered	Total
(1-9 copies)	$ 16.95	_____	_____
(10-24 copies)	12.95	_____	_____
(25-49 copies)	11.45	_____	_____
(50 -100 copies)	9.95	_____	_____

Shipping and Handling
1st book	$ 3.00		
each additional	$ 1.00		_____
(maximum S&H $15.00)			

TOTAL ENCLOSED _____

SEND CHECK OR MONEY ORDER TO:
John Breeding
2503 Douglas Street
Austin, TX 78741
(512) 326-8326